Gifts

Gifts

TRUE STORIES OF GOD'S LOVE

AS RETOLD BY

LARRY BARKDULL

DESERET
BOOK

SALT LAKE CITY, UTAH

Library of Congress Cataloging-in-Publication Data

Barkdull, Larry.
   Gifts : true stories of God's love.   Larry Barkdull.
      p.   cm.
   ISBN 1-59038-212-9 (pbk.)
   1. Christian life—Mormon authors.   2. Miracles.   I. Title.
   BX8656.B36   2004
   242—dc22
                                                  2003026589

Printed in the United States of America   18961-7158
R.R. Donnelley and Sons, Crawfordsville, IN

10 9 8 7 6 5 4 3 2 1

Fear thou not;

for I am with thee:

Be not dismayed;

for I am thy God:

I will strengthen thee; yea,

I will help thee; yea,

I will uphold thee

(ISAIAH 41:10)

Contents

Introduction 1

THE GIVER

When the Answer Was No 11

Becoming Acquainted with God 14

POWER OF GOD

Saved from AIDS and Kidney Failure 19

Falling off the Roof on Halloween Night 26

In God's Time, but in Plenty of Time 29

When the Skin Graft Failed 31

Amputation! 33

O Ye of Little Faith 36

A Righteous Example of Faith 39

The Last Obstacle 41

To Unstop the Ears of the Deaf 44

Calming the Storms 47

Contents

A Simple Prayer 49

Burned! 51

A Gift of Tongues 55

Knowledge of God

The Rusty Bucket of Rainwater 61

Head-on Collision 63

In a Flicker of Time 65

The Lord's Lost-and-Found Department 67

In an Instant 70

To Listen Carefully 74

Fifty Dollars 77

Twice Protected 79

One Cab in 20,000 84

Ask, Fast, and Go 87

Tornado 89

Cut the Rope! 91

Don't Plan Anything 93

Love of God

For the First Time, I Saw a Bird 99

No Food in the House 101

Praying for an Accident 103

Lost, but Not Forgotten 107

Contents

Turning Away from the Bunkhouse
and the Cowboy 116

Miracle at Sea 118

The Miracle of a Mother's Love 123

Praying for Your Enemies 125

Rescued Onboard Ship 130

Two Navajo Women of Faith 133

A Good Trade 138

Welcome Home 140

THE POWER, KNOWLEDGE, AND LOVE OF GOD
A Story That Must Be Told 145

Introduction

In the springtime of the early 1930s, a young Argentine lad received an unexpected gift—a miracle. I interviewed him years later when he was an old man. He recalled his life-altering experience.

"My father had charged me with the responsibility of leading his horses from a high mountain corral through an open pasture to a lower corral. En route, something spooked the herd and they began to stampede down the mountain. I ran after them, but I was too small to catch them."

"What did you do?" I asked.

"I fell to my knees and pled with God to help me."

"What happened?"

"Some men suddenly came out of the woods and caught the horses . . . *and I have never believed in God since.*"

I was stunned. "But what an obvious gift from God!" I said.

"It wasn't God," he countered. "It was those *men* that caught the horses. God had nothing to do with it."

I departed shaking my head. But over the years I have come to judge that man less harshly. On occasion I, too, have rigidly set my sights on receiving a specific gift and failed to recognize the Giver.

Sadly, some people explain away their gifts as strokes of good luck while other people overlook their gifts completely. Humble observers, on the other hand, attest to the continuous generosity of an unseen Giver who has often intervened in times of crisis when other options have failed. Simply put, they recognize that they received an unmistakable gift.

Gifts, by definition, are pure, voluntary offerings of love, indisputable evidence of the giver's affection. Gifts cannot be *earned;* they are freely imparted with no expectation of repayment. Every gift uniquely reflects something of the giver's personality. The gifts of God, for example, reveal his attributes of character, including his power, his awareness, and his love. In *Lectures on Faith,* the Prophet Joseph Smith stated that faith pivots on our hope and belief that God possesses these and other characteristics in absolute perfection. In times of urgency, we *hope* that God has the power to help; we *hope* that he is aware of us; and we *hope* that he loves us enough to stand by us and lead us to a solution. We reach out to the Giver and plead for his gifts because we believe that he has both the ability and the disposition to grant them. We believe that he is a perfect being who possesses an unchangeable set of attributes and characteristics upon which we can completely rely. The following is an adapted list of these attributes and characteristics, along with some personal commentary, inspired by Joseph Smith's *Lectures on Faith.*

POWER. God is all-powerful. Otherwise, how could I believe that he could help me if I imagined that something was beyond his ability? Nothing is too hard for him. He can do anything, in any situation, at any time, in my behalf.

KNOWLEDGE. God possesses all knowledge about everything, including past, present, and future events. Otherwise, how could I believe that he could anticipate and solve my problems if there were something that he didn't know, or if his attention were momentarily diverted from me, or if I thought he had forgotten me? He intimately knows and *foreknows* me and is constantly aware of my thoughts and my circumstances.

LOVE. I am God's child. I have all his attention all of the time. He loves me completely. He is merciful, compassionate, kind, comforting, patient, gracious, and abundant in goodness. Otherwise, how could I seek his help to face unbearable situations or to take the difficult steps of change if anything I was going through or had done could distance me from his love? His love for me is unconditional and continual, and it is the consistent motivating force in his interactions with me.

CONSISTENCY. God is perfectly unchangeable. What he did yesterday he will be doing today and tomorrow. Otherwise, how could I anticipate what whims or circumstances might change his mercy to reproach or his love to hatred?

JUSTICE. God is perfectly equitable and no respecter of persons. Otherwise, how could I believe in him if I thought that he played favorites? If God's laws specify blessings and consequences, I can count on his justice to prevail and his judgment to be correct.

TRUTH. God cannot lie. He does not make promises casually. Otherwise, how could I believe that my future with him is secure if

I thought that he didn't mean what he said or that he might change his mind? He will keep his word in his own way and in his own time.

When the events of our lives shake the foundation of our faith and we find it cracked and shifting, we should ask ourselves: "Which of these characteristics do I believe that God lacks?"

Ultimately, faith is measured, strengthened, and injured by our level of belief that the Giver possesses these attributes in total perfection. And even a little belief on our part seems to be enough to receive his gifts. For example, a child may not completely comprehend his earthly father, but that does not prevent that father from showering gifts of loving care upon the child. That affectionate attention teaches the child to trust his father. A more mature understanding will come. Time is on the father's side. Many and varied experiences and the giving of many gifts will establish a solid foundation of understanding and trust. With each experience the child recognizes more fully that his father loves him and nothing that the child does can change that fact. The gifts continue to come. The child learns that he can depend on his father's reaction and stability of character, and that even his most trivial problem will be considered significant. The father and the child come to know one another best during hard times when they must make sacrifices for each other. How else can love and loyalty be proven? At some point in the relationship the child matures and suddenly has a burst of understanding: All that his father has ever given and done was motivated by love. No *quid pro quo*—no this for that. Everything was a gift.

The gifts of God are unique in that they are inexplicable by the laws of nature. We recipients cannot replicate them. Their existence should point our attention to the Giver. We may try to explain them away, but we shouldn't. We may not immediately recognize them, but we should try. We may carelessly forget them, but that may prove to be a serious mistake. The fabric of the Book of Mormon is woven with the thread *Remember*.

The gifts of God attest of his nearness and his interest in our welfare. Elder Neal A. Maxwell has said, "God is found in the details of our lives." Thus, we not only expect to find the Giver drawing near during our struggles with relationships, finances, health, and weaknesses, but we also expect to find him whispering comfort and instruction in our secret prayers, quietly teaching us during scripture study, and walking and talking with us "in the cool of the day" (Genesis 3:8). We encounter him as we labor over difficult decisions, and we feel his presence as he gently urges us to do and be better. We find the Giver warning us of danger, providing us with strength to endure, and pointing out carefully prepared paths of escape. We glimpse him delivering unexpected bouquets of affection, those almost anonymous offerings that communicate: "I am aware. I am near. I love you."

The Giver's gifts are individualized. No good purpose is served by comparing our gifts with those enjoyed by others. *This happened to me and not him; this happened to him and not me.* "For all have not every gift given unto them; for there are many gifts, and to every man is given a gift by the Spirit of God" (D&C 46:11). Although we collectively may share a common destination, our paths to it are as strikingly diverse as are the gifts that mark our ways. All this bespeaks a Giver who is remarkably personal. With distance comes insight, and one day we will discover that the distribution of his gifts was fair after all.

The *fairness* issue leads to a harder one. A risk in compiling a book of miracles is fielding the difficult question: *In my time of need, where was my miracle?* I am not so bold as to suggest that I know. Prophets, statesmen, philosophers, and great leaders also wondered as they cried out for deliverance and were not spared the extremes of life. That their faith ultimately sustained them, however, despite seeming contradictions, and that they did not abandon God are the very reasons that we honor them. Their *nondeliverance* often proved to be the greatest miracle of their lives, for it was during their deep search for meaning that they made a decision to continue to trust God at every hazard, even when the outcome seemed contrary to their belief in him. "Though he slay me, yet will I trust in him" (Job 13:15). We do not make heroes of people who have never been through anything. We know the histories of the heroes, and we know that they were not forgotten after all. The promise is given and God cannot lie: "I will not forsake you." When God does not readily answer, it does not mean he can't or won't or is indifferent or unaware. He must have a purpose and that purpose is always motivated by love. "He doeth not anything save it be for the benefit of the world [for the benefit of me] . . ." (2 Nephi 26:24).

God is not in the business of destroying faith. There is absolutely no risk in trusting him. The one certainty in uncertainty is that perspective will come and that all things will work together for our good. God insists on it. Seasons pass—after winter comes spring. Just so, adversity must yield to good fortune. But our definition of deliverance is not always God's definition. We can dictate neither timelines nor terms. But we do know that he is the Deliverer and he makes no apology for that title. We are certain that he cares for us dearly and that he will walk beside us and before us until he has subdued all our enemies under his feet (see D&C 76:61) and until he has wiped away all our tears (see Revelation 7:17).

Gifts is a collection of real-life experiences. When exceptional help was needed, a gift was given and evidence of the existence of the Giver became clear. The stories in *Gifts* demonstrate that we can be absolutely confident that our every prayer is heard and counts, and that somewhere in the process of *working through,* a divine encounter will happen and the divine character attributes of the Giver will be revealed. Furthermore, the stories were precipitated by need. I interviewed no one who said he or she had discovered God when things were going well. To a person, each received his or her gift as a *result* of adversity. Something extraordinary needed to happen and often did. These stories are meant to provide hope, anchor faith, and affirm that prayers are heard and answers come. They are intended to be messages of hope that communicate, "Hold on your way. The miracle is still before you. Trust God to reveal it to you. Trust in the perfection of his attributes of character. Somewhere along your journey, you will come to know him."

Each story in this collection is told in the voice of the person to whom it happened. Because of the sacred nature of their experiences, some of the contributors desired to share their stories anonymously and to this end changed the names of participants.

To a person, the contributors considered their experience *holy ground* whereon they became better acquainted with God and his attributes of character. They believe that their hope is anchored to something substantial. They believe they are not alone. It is upon our own *holy ground* that we readers add our stories to theirs. It is upon our own *holy ground* that we become acquainted with the Giver, who hears us, who knows us, who has the ability to help us, and who loves us enough to shower us with his gifts.

The Giver

Thanks be unto God for his unspeakable gift.

2 Corinthians 9:15

When the Answer Was No

When Mother was dying of cancer, she asked for a priesthood blessing to know the will of the Lord and, if possible, to be healed. I agreed to give the blessing, but I knew it would be the hardest of my life. Not that it would be harder for the Lord. I knew that he could heal cancer as easily as a cold. But for me, I had to prepare. I dared not approach this blessing casually.

Over the next few days, I attended the temple and prayed and humbled myself before the Lord. I read the scriptures about miraculous manifestations of power and healing. I counseled with wise men who had spent a lifetime exercising their priesthood righteously. Then I began to fast. I would not eat until after the blessing had been given.

Mother lived six hours away. As I drove through the night, I prayed continuously. I attempted to remove all doubt from my mind. I knew that God could heal her; I knew that the priesthood was the designated power, and I knew that the ordinance of anointing and sealing had been revealed for this very purpose. I had prepared to a point of confidence and clarity. I pushed aside the temptation to craft words and *plan* the blessing. I had no desire to be eloquent or clever. I only wanted to plainly state what would be dictated by the inspiration of the Spirit—and remarkably, I now felt fully prepared to pronounce the promise of healing and to witness its miracle.

I will not describe my reaction as I stepped into Mother's room and witnessed her frail, weakened body. My emotions were so tender. I loved my mother. How I longed for divine permission to pronounce the words of healing. Our family knelt in prayer. We pled for a miracle. I was sure it would come.

It did.

At the moment I laid my hands upon my mother's head, the Spirit said, "No."

I wasn't prepared for the answer. But I felt Mother relax and concede under my hands. The miracle followed—sweet words of comfort and peace, every word dictated by a loving influence that knew her and understood her pain. Mom was going home.

When the answer is "no" or "not now," or when the answer comes in minute steps that require protracted endurance, we can draw comfort from the account of the Savior in Gethsemane:

"And he was withdrawn from them about a stone's cast, and kneeled down, and prayed, Saying, Father, if thou be willing, remove this cup from me: nevertheless not my will, but thine, be done. *And there appeared an angel unto him from heaven, strengthening him* (Luke 22:41–43).

What I discovered through this tender experience is that God may say no and allow us to suffer for a season, but that suffering will ultimately be of some benefit. In the meantime, he will never leave us without comfort. We can fully expect to receive heavenly help to give us the strength to face one more day. Often miracles come in the form of a feeling of peace in the midst of turbulence or an increased capacity to endure when the odds seem staggering or it feels impossible to sweat out the Gethsemanes of our lives.

❧

Father, if thou be willing, remove this cup from me:
nevertheless not my will, but thine, be done.

LUKE 22:42

Becoming Acquainted with God

The oft-told tale of the ill-fated journey of the Martin and Willie handcart companies provides an example of faith and endurance. Having begun their westward trek late in the fall of 1856, these determined pioneers were caught in an early winter storm in Wyoming. Although help was quickly dispatched from Salt Lake City, the storm took a terrible toll. Some people froze to death; others starved. That any survived was a miracle; for many souls, deliverance never came.

Later when the survivors had recovered in the safety of the Salt Lake Valley, they settled on farms and tried to piece together their lives. Years of controversy ensued. Debating the wisdom of their late-season journey made good fodder for backyard courts and juries. Much later, in the setting of a comfortable, frontier Sunday School class, criticism was once again raised about the leaders' shortsightedness in attempting the trek so late in the year.

An old man in the corner sat silently and listened as long as he could stand it, then he arose and said things that no person who heard him will ever forget. His face was white with emotion, yet he spoke calmly, deliberately, but with great earnestness and sincerity.

In substance he said, "I ask you to stop this criticism. You are discussing a matter you know nothing about. Cold historic facts mean nothing here for they give no proper interpretation of the questions involved. A mistake to send the handcart company out so late in the season? Yes. But I was in that company and my wife was in it. . . . We suffered beyond anything you can imagine and many died of exposure and starvation, but did you ever hear a survivor of that company utter a word of criticism? Not one of that company ever apostatized or left the Church because every one of us came through with the absolute knowledge that God lives, for we became acquainted with him in our extremities" (Gordon B. Hinckley, "Our Mission of Saving," *Ensign,* Nov. 1991, 54).

Peace be unto thy soul; thine adversity and thine afflictions shall be but a small moment; And then, if thou endure it well, God shall exalt thee on high.

D&C 121:7–8

Power of God

With God all things are possible.

MATTHEW 19:26

Saved from AIDS and Kidney Failure

On April 1, 1990, my wife and I rushed our fifteen-year-old son, Matt, to the hospital because he was bleeding internally. The next day we were told that he had end-stage renal disease—kidney failure. For an unknown reason his kidneys had stopped functioning. Initially we thought that the internal bleeding was due to his having been born with hemophilia, an inherited blood disorder. Compared to a normal person, Matt produces less than one percent of the blood-clotting agent. His type of hemophilia is considered severe.

Our concern over Matt's hemorrhaging was the latest in a long list of health problems. But we had hope. Some years earlier, a medical breakthrough had promised a dramatic lifestyle change for the hemophiliac community—*Factor*. Researchers had developed a method of isolating and extracting the deficient coagulant in the blood. Now home infusions to coagulate blood could be administered in minutes rather than in hours at the hospital. But we were about to discover that as marvelous as was this life-saving Factor, it had a deadly side effect. At that time, few of us knew that the blood pool was contaminated with the HIV virus. In fact, during the

1980s, fully 95 percent of hemophiliacs who had received Factor became infected. Most would eventually die of AIDS. As information trickled down to us, the frightening possibility that Matt might have AIDS became a concern. Over the years, Matt had watched friends with whom he had attended hemophilia camp contract HIV and develop full-blown AIDS and die. My wife's hemophiliac cousin had been one of the casualties. As examples of innocent populations being decimated by plagues, one is reminded of the diseases that the white man brought to the Hawaiians and the American Indians. For hemophiliacs, the very medicine that they needed to stay alive was killing them!

But to fully tell our story, I must step back in time.

I had spent much of 1987 consumed with the impression that Matt was in danger, but I did not know why. Hemophilia? AIDS? Something else? All I knew was he needed protection through a priesthood blessing. As I stated, there was very little information available about the HIV hazard at that time; and we, of course, had no idea that his kidneys were in the slow process of failing. I continued to have the continuous nagging impression that Matt's life was or would be in peril, and I began to pray for guidance. I fasted; I attended the temple; I made the subject a matter of ongoing contemplation.

One night, after nine months' effort to receive inspiration, I was reading Alma, chapter 7, where Alma explains how Christ has suffered for all of our afflictions. Suddenly, understanding burst upon my mind: *Matt's afflictions had already been faced and overcome in the*

Atonement. The keys to Matt's survival were now with Christ, if we could gain permission to access them.

I suddenly felt a sense of both confidence and urgency. Matt could be protected and healed by an appeal to the Savior, but he needed a priesthood blessing *now!* Actual words for the petition came to my mind. I immediately called upon two men of extraordinary faith and experience to help with the anointing and sealing. We all prepared as best we could. Then, on a designated evening, we knelt together in prayer and pled for divine consent to turn specific keys of the Atonement in Matt's behalf. The experience was powerful. Promises of protection, healing, and long life were pronounced. A record was made of the blessing. We were at peace.

Over the next few years, Matt continued to receive Factor as more and more information was being gathered about hemophiliacs' contracting the AIDS virus. Our greatest scare came late one night when we received an urgent phone call warning us to avoid a certain batch of Factor because it had been contaminated with HIV. Only hours earlier, we had given Matt an injection of that medicine. (Today, hemophilia medicines are subjected to heat treatments and freezing to ensure their purity. Now, becoming infected with the AIDS virus is a remote possibility.)

The miracle? Matt never did contract HIV, although his doctors confirm that he was exposed to it. The physicians were perplexed and asked for samples of his "rare" blood to help in HIV research. It didn't help them. Obviously, the effects of a priesthood blessing cannot be seen under a microscope. We felt blessed. Heavenly Father had sent us a warning and a solution. We had witnessed a miracle, but we had no comprehension of the priesthood blessing's far-reaching effects. We would be the participants in more miracles.

April 2, 1990–The day after Matt had begun to hemorrhage internally, my wife and I arrived at the hospital only to be rushed into a quiet room by a doctor who told us that Matt's kidneys had failed. The doctor couldn't understand why Matt wasn't in a coma. My wife and I were devastated. We were suddenly faced with the very real possibility that our son might die. Reaching out for help, I phoned my father-in-law and our bishop to help me give a blessing. During the two hours that we waited for them to arrive, I walked the hospital grounds weeping and praying for peace. But nothing came. Finally, I arrived at a decision: No matter what happened, I would allow nothing to turn me away from God. I would trust him. I said aloud, "If you must take my son, it will be hard for me, but I won't stop believing in you."

Later, as we priesthood holders gathered around Matt's bed, Grandpa offered a blessing of healing. His eloquent words acknowledged a power beyond our own, and he pled that that power be invoked in Matt's behalf. When he finished, I stepped back to the far side of the room as loved ones stood by Matt and talked to him. Then our bishop turned and walked toward me. Placing his hands on both of my shoulders, he looked me squarely in the eyes and said, "Matt will be all right." His words shot through me like lightning, and something like a voice spoke to my mind as if to say, "That is right!"

For the next three months our family life was put on hold as my wife and I took tests to see which of us might be able to donate a kidney. Dialysis was now keeping Matt alive. We were soon to discover that becoming a donor was not an easy task. One must be in prime health and have no previous history of serious illness. After taking a particular test, the doctors told me that I could not be considered as a donor because at age eleven I had contracted nephritis, a complication of strep infection that attacks the kidneys. At that young age, I had nearly died . . . of kidney failure! The doctors told me that my kidneys had surely been damaged. They rejected me! Strangely, some months earlier, before Matt's kidney failure, I had followed the story of Senator Jake Garn's donating a kidney to his daughter. The Spirit had then whispered to me: "One day you will do that too." It was a strange impression that I had tried to dismiss, only to have it surface again and again. Now, in the middle of donor tests, it felt like a clear directive. I was not about to be told by doctors that I could not be considered as a donor.

On the day that I was rejected, I drove home concerned that the burden of donating a kidney would fall to my wife. I was confused about the former impression that I had received and I began to pray vocally. Suddenly, the thought came into my mind, *Go ask your bishop for a blessing, and your kidneys will be fine.*

I obeyed.

I immediately drove to the Bishop's house and explained my feelings. He listened. He understood. He prayed. He laid his hands on my head and implored God to intervene. Later, I returned to the hospital and begged the doctors to allow me to continue to take the donor tests alongside my wife. They relented, but held out little hope. No former nephritic patient had ever donated a kidney, they said. For that matter, only one other hemophiliac had ever received a donated kidney. From the onset, our case would be rare, if not improbable.

For the next month, my wife and I endured a barrage of donor tests. Then the result came. My kidneys were perfect! I was chosen to be the donor.

The next sets of tests were difficult and invasive. One test revealed that I had been born with WPW Syndrome, a rare heart condition that affects one in 100,000 people. An extra electrical pathway to the heart causes periodic palpitations. I could be on the operating table, I was told, and my heart might suffer an arrhythmia and I could die. The transplant date was put on hold.

As I prayed for guidance, I received an impression *once again* to ask for a blessing from my bishop, and *once again* my bishop humbly laid his hands upon my head and petitioned God for help. When I left his office, I had a feeling of peace, and I returned to the hospital to undergo extensive tests on my heart. The results came a week later. "You *do* have WPW," said a voice on the phone, "but it doesn't appear to be serious enough to stop you from donating." A new transplant date was set, and I entered the final phase of donor testing. That phase would include an angiogram.

"Your *plumbing* is abnormal," a doctor told me as he studied the results of the angiogram.

"Abnormal?" I was stunned.

Abnormal proved to be an understatement. A *normal* kidney has attached to it one vein and one artery. In my case, one of my kidneys had two veins and two arteries and the other kidney had two veins and three arteries! This situation posed at least two problems: How would the doctors reroute everything inside me? And how would the doctors splice into Matt a kidney that had too many holes?

This time the transplant plans came to a complete halt. Specialists from around the country were consulted. In the meantime, our family did the only thing we could do: We went to our knees. Once again, our bishop was our answer. In our time of need, and for the third time, he laid his hands on my head and pled for an outpouring of inspiration to be with the doctors as they weighed the options. Again, we felt peace. When the call came a week later, no explanation was given. The transplant office at the hospital simply said, "Everything is on for July third. They will take your left kidney."

Today Matt is married and has two daughters. He has received his master's degree in marriage and family therapy and is helping others through their difficulties in life.

One night in 1990, in a dark hospital room, I sat with Matt as he was suffering from a high fever, the result of yet another complication due to his failed kidneys. He thought that he couldn't take any more and he wondered out loud if there was a God, or if God existed, why he would allow such suffering. The profound answer to Matt's question came quietly and convincingly. Beyond all the miracles that had and would result from priesthood blessings and treatments, in a very private way, in the crucible of adversity, Matt found his God who would provide him healing and see him through.

❧

For with God nothing shall be impossible.

LUKE 1:37

Falling off the Roof on Halloween Night

Years ago, my son Jon (name changed) and his friends, then teenagers, had tired of trick-or-treating. One of the boys was the son of my friend Ted. His roof could easily be climbed and often was. It required little effort for a nimble 16-year-old boy to mount the fence, swing a leg up, and roll onto the roof.

Looking for more excitement that boring Halloween night, the boys had climbed to the peak of Ted's roof and pondered the possibilities. Someone suggested that they rig a microphone to scare passing trick-or-treaters. There were no dissenters. The prank played out like this: Target a victim below, scream into the microphone, and run to another side of the roof to hide. Their fun time went on for a long time.

The boys had just frightened another unsuspecting child and had raced to the far, dark side of the roof, when suddenly Jon disappeared. His friends heard a hard thump twelve feet below. When I received a phone call from Ted, he could only say, "Jon's been hurt. It's pretty bad."

I arrived just as an ambulance was pulling up. My son was lying on his back, unconscious and groaning. When the paramedics shined a flashlight on him, I saw blood seeping from his ears.

"He fell directly onto his head and right shoulder," one of them said. I tried to reach out for him but was prevented. "He may have injured his neck or back," they said.

Anticipating my need for a friend, Ted said, "I'll go with you to the emergency room."

At the hospital, doctors cut away Jon's shirt and began to work on him. Nothing could have prepared me for the sight. He was still bleeding from his ears. His face was swelling. There was a large lump on his right collarbone that looked as though the bone might suddenly poke through the skin. I was told that it was severely broken.

"Does the bleeding from the ears mean head injury?" I asked.

"It's the sign of concussion. It doesn't look good."

"What about his neck and back?"

"We've ordered a CAT scan."

When the doctors left the room, I said to Ted, "I'm so afraid for my son. Will you help me give him a priesthood blessing?"

Ted is a man of great faith. Over the years, he and I had been each other's home teachers. We had given many blessings together. In other trying situations, I had seen him take his problems to the Lord with the perfect assurance that he would be heard and answered. On occasion, I had knelt with him and heard him pour out his heart in behalf of someone in need. This was to be another of those times. We stood on either side of my son's bed and pled for a miracle of healing. Then we laid our hands on my son's head and pronounced the blessing. When we finished, the doctors took Jon to Radiology.

During that long night while we watched Jon's unconscious body being scanned, we talked of God, faith, and past miracles. I didn't know what would happen to my boy. Periodically I called home to discuss the situation with my wife, who was tending our younger children. We tried to prepare ourselves for whatever news might come. Finally, a doctor came from a room and approached Ted and me with a handful of X rays. His speech was clinical. He pointed out bones, growth plates, and the obvious concussion.

"Has the bleeding from the ears stopped?" I asked. "Is there any brain damage?"

"The bleeding has stopped and there is no apparent brain damage."

"What about breaks? His back, his neck?"

"No breaks."

"Not even his collar bone?" I asked in astonishment.

"Nothing. He will probably have a headache for a few days."

Jon woke up twenty-four hours later with the predicted headache, not remembering anything except standing on the edge of the dark roof. The bruising and swelling was gone within the week. Within a few days, he was back playing *carefully* with his friends.

❧

The Lord is good, a strong hold in the day of trouble;
and he knoweth them that trust in him.

NAHUM 1:7

In God's Time, but in Plenty of Time

December of 1984 was filled with dark days. Never had my wife and I had more cause to question our decision to have a large family. To the continuing cost of diapers was added the expenses of old cars that barely held together. Our two clunkers had devoured the few dollars we had managed to save for emergencies and now had begun to consume the resources we needed for food and other family basics. One car needed a replacement radiator and water pump. The transmission had died in the other. Both needed new batteries. And it was December—Christmas!

We could see no relief from our monetary crisis.

My teaching job was rewarding in many ways, but not necessarily financially. We had always walked on the edge of financial solvency. For some years, my wife had been providing a daytime babysitting service to help meet expenses. Recently, the mother of one of the children told us she could not bring her child anymore, meaning that we would lose another $200 per month. But the automobile problems were the setbacks that devastated us.

As much as we had tried, we could not find a way to make our money stretch. Finally, there was no place to turn but to God. Kneeling together, my wife and I implored him to intervene. We told him of our need and our belief that he could help us. In the following days we were amazed at his willingness and ability to bless us. Within the next seven days:

1) A friend at work gave me $100. Someone had given it to him with the provision that he should give it to a family in need. He wasn't sure why, but my family had come to his mind.

2) My brother handed me $100. "Here," he said. "I think you need this."

3) My mother sent us $50. She said she had a little extra that month.

4) A friend wrote me a check for $500. He said someone had helped him years before and now it was time to pass on the blessings.

5) Another friend hired me for a few days' work in the afternoons and paid me $150.

6) A local college called to ask if I could teach a class beginning in January. The pay: $1,375.

I had never discussed my financial situation with any of these people. In one week from the moment of that prayer, God provided us with $2,275—enough for the cars and Christmas—from sources we never expected. The miracle came in God's time, but in plenty of time.

❧

And I know, O Lord, that thou hast all power, and can do whatsoever thou wilt for the benefit of man.

ETHER 3:4

When the Skin Graft Failed

At the age of thirteen, I underwent *another* in a series of very painful skin grafting surgeries to correct complications of a third-degree burn from my childhood. By now I knew the healing procedure well. After the operation, the skin graft would need several weeks to bond to my body. I was to stay down and not do anything too strenuous.

At that time I was in a dance group that was preparing to go to Florida to perform at Walt Disney World. I knew that if I didn't rehearse, I wouldn't be allowed to perform. I pled with my mother to let me go to rehearsal, but my begging didn't convince her. However, I had age on my side. I was thirteen and had already figured out what all teenagers eventually figure out: Persistence pays. So I employed tears and groaning and tried to wear her down. "If you will just let me attend rehearsal," I told her, "I won't do anything except *watch*."

Mom reluctantly gave in.

Needless to say, I didn't just watch; I danced. I was afraid that if I didn't, I wouldn't be allowed to go on the trip. I was in terrible pain, but I participated in the rehearsal.

Later that evening, as I loosened the bandages to change my surgical dressing, I suddenly felt a tremendous burning and throbbing around the graft. As I peeled away the gauze, the recently grafted skin came off with it! A gaping wound on my chest was oozing blood and pus. Probably the combination of the seeing the injury and feeling the pain caused me to faint. When my parents heard the crash, they quickly found me and carried me to my bed. Realizing the seriousness of the situation, they knelt beside me, offered an urgent prayer, and then my father gave me a blessing.

I later awoke in the doctor's office. Even though I had fallen unconscious, I had somehow managed to press the graft to my chest with a hand. Now my arm felt frozen in place. I expected the doctor to say that I would need another painful surgery. However, when he removed my hand and examined the graft, all the skin had reattached except for a tiny piece, which he stapled in place. Everything else had completely healed.

Soon thereafter, I was able to go with my dance group to Disney World. I will be forever grateful for my parents, who in spite of their thirteen-year-old daughter's irresponsible behavior, asked the Lord to bless me. Their wonderful example of faith and trust in God's power has stayed with me through the years.

❧

Know ye not that ye are in the hands of God?
Know ye not that he hath all power?
MORMON 5:23

Amputation!

One of the things that I miss most about my husband being gone is holding hands with him. It has now been almost six years since his death, and I still find myself instinctively reaching for his steadying, comforting hand.

We were walking hand-in-hand one day on our way to the Manila Philippines Temple, where we were serving as missionaries. Suddenly my husband's leg began to cramp and he almost fell. He quickly reached out for me to steady himself and then began to massage the leg vigorously. After achieving a measure of relief, he was able to hobble to the temple to go to work. Throughout the day, he rubbed and favored his cramping leg.

The leg vexed him for days to come. "Old age," he would complain as he tried to work through the pain and continue his assignment in the temple. Previous experiences had soured him on the local medical care, so he had decided to wait until we returned home from our mission to consult his regular doctors.

My husband had had a history of heart problems, and after we returned to the United States, he entered the hospital for an extensive series of X rays and CAT scans in search of the cause of his recurring leg cramps. One day, after undergoing a battery of tests, he was wheeled into a hallway because the hospital was crowded and no recovery rooms were available. As he lay on the gurney, I held his hand and waited. Soon, a medical professional approached us carrying film.

"What's the prognosis?" my husband asked.

"A blockage at your knee," was the reply. "Veins, arteries—all blocked off."

"What can be done?"

"There is a bypass procedure, but it's experimental."

"And if that doesn't work?"

"We'll just have to lop it off." With those words, the professional made slicing motion with his arm as though it were a guillotine. Having delivered this chilling message, he walked away without emotion, as though this were commonplace news that he was used to offering.

My husband fell into an immediate and deep depression. *Lop it off!* That meant amputation at the knee. My husband was an organist and a temple worker. How would he play? How would he work? We checked out of the hospital and went home discouraged and frightened. It was obvious that the medical community did not have a solution.

Compounded by the man's decidedly poor bedside manner, the message was frighteningly clear: In order to save my husband's life, his leg would have to be sacrificed. No earthly skill seemed to be available to save the leg. We now knew that only an appeal to God could help.

We called for the elders, two trusted friends. In tears my husband explained to them the diagnosis, then he asked, "Will you bless me?"

All of us dedicated a day to prepare for the blessing. We prayed, fasted, and took our petition to the temple. That evening, we met together to pray again and seek the Lord's intervention. Then the holy ordinance of anointing was performed, followed by the sealing, in which these inspired words were uttered: "Let the blood, the life-giving blood, course through your veins and reach into every part of your body."

Thereafter, we sought another doctor's advice. After he had conducted more tests, we met for consultation. It was true, he said, the veins and arteries at the knee were irreversibly clogged . . . but he could feel a faint pulse in the toes! The leg was yet alive!

"How can it be?" we asked.

"Somehow your body has set up an alternate circulation system, and the blood is being carried through your leg by the capillaries."

"And the amputation?"

"You will not lose your leg!"

That day I think we held hands more tightly than we ever had before. We held hands and *walked* out of the doctor's office, grateful to God for his kindness and intervention. For ten more wonderful years, we continued to hold hands and walk together.

❧

Behold, I am from above, and my power lieth beneath. I am over all, and in all, and through all, and search all things, and the day cometh that all things shall be subject unto me. Behold, I am Alpha and Omega, even Jesus Christ.

D&C 63:59–60

O Ye of Little Faith

One Friday afternoon I was paged to the emergency room of the hospital where I was serving as the hospital chaplain. Doctors were frantically working on a gentleman who had just suffered a massive stroke. Soon, four of the man's family members arrived, screaming, wailing, and sobbing, each accusing the others of causing the stroke. I realized immediately that this was going to be one of my more challenging cases.

After the man was taken into surgery, I ushered the family into a separate room and spoke to them at length, trying to calm them. Then I told them I would try to find out what was happening in the operating room. Before I could leave them, however, the man's wife asked if I would offer a prayer for her husband. I agreed. We bowed our heads and I began to speak. During the prayer, something incredible happened: I felt prompted to promise that the man would recover. When I ended the prayer and looked up, I could see that the family's countenance had noticeably brightened. Then a shock of anxiety shot through me. I excused myself and headed for Surgery.

When I saw the physicians emerging, removing their surgical hats and gloves, I could tell from the expression on their faces that the prognosis was bleak. The man had indeed suffered a massive stroke, and the surgeons said that there was no hope of recovery. The term "vegetable" was used. Then the words of my prayer began to haunt me. I was a professional; I knew better than to feed loved ones false hope. I also knew how volatile and emotionally frail this family was. I began to concoct a plan to amend the things I had said in the prayer. At length I decided that I would relate what the doctors had said about the man's condition and suggest that we have another prayer. During the prayer I would set the record straight. I would be careful to say nothing about recovering.

When I visited with the family again, I did not have to suggest another prayer; they requested it! They said they had been so comforted by my first prayer that they wanted me to pray for their husband and father again. I swallowed hard and obliged. During the prayer I struggled to choose my words carefully. I thought I was doing fine until I was once again prompted to repeat the promise of recovery. I looked up to smiles and relief. My dilemma was increasing: I knew that I had received promptings, but I also knew what the doctors were saying. I politely excused myself and headed toward the recovery room to learn from the seasoned nurses about this man's true condition.

"Terminal," I was told. "It is just a matter of time."

I felt sick inside. I was confused. I returned to the family and stayed with them until the man was moved to Intensive Care. Late that Friday afternoon, when it was time for me to go home, I summoned the courage to ask the family if I could once more offer a prayer. They agreed, and, as I bowed my head, I thought to myself,

Now is your last opportunity to clarify this man's situation and prepare the family for the inevitable. Whatever you do, don't say he is going to recover from this stroke!

But I couldn't follow through. To my dismay I felt prompted to make the same promise. Dismayed, I left for home assuming that by the time I returned on Monday morning the man would have died.

I had no peaceful weekend. I was nervous. I was more nervous when I returned to work on Monday. Would the man have passed away? Would his family be distraught? When I approached the front desk I tentatively checked the roster, and amazingly the man was still alive and in Intensive Care.

His wife and a son greeted me, and together we stepped into the man's room and to his bedside.

"He is still in a coma," his wife whispered, "but we are so comforted by your prayers. Would you mind offering another one here?"

I agreed and prayed as she had requested and, for the fourth time, the same words of assurance flowed from my mouth. I had no sooner finished than the man opened his eyes, sat up in bed, looked at his son said, "What are you smiling at, knucklehead?"

I walked out of the room and said to myself, "O ye of little faith."

❧

The Lord of hosts hath sworn, saying, Surely as I have thought,
so shall it come to pass; and as I have purposed, so shall
it stand: . . . who shall disannul it? and his hand is
stretched out, and who shall turn it back?

ISAIAH 14:24, 27

A Righteous Example of Faith

I had just received my mission call when my father had a heart attack and was admitted to the hospital. He had recently ordained me an elder. He now requested that I bring a family friend and come to the hospital to give him a blessing. I called a man who had served with my father in the branch presidency. En route to the hospital, it never occurred to me that I would be asked to seal; I fully expected this friend to give the blessing. When we arrived, however, much to my surprise, the friend announced that he would anoint and I would seal.

After the friend had anointed my father, he coached me in sealing the anointing. Then, when it came time for me to pronounce a blessing, I scanned my memory for a model. I had witnessed my father perform this ordinance many times, and I remembered how straightforwardly he spoke when he administered to people. I remembered when my younger sister had contracted polio and he had blessed her. The disease progressed so seriously that she had lost the use of her legs and had ended up in an iron lung. After she had been in that situation for a few months, my father decided that the physicians had done all they could, so he went to the hospital full of faith and with the authority of the priesthood. He told the doctors that he was going to take his daughter out of the iron lung and take her home that day. A young intern said, "If you take her out of the iron lung she will die."

My father was not deterred. He gave my sister a priesthood blessing, then asked the doctors to remove her from the iron lung. The young intern was reluctant, but removed her and carefully began to exercise her legs. As the intern took the soles of her feet in his hands, he pushed her legs up against her chest and asked if she could push back against his hands. She responded by kicking him up against the wall! Then she got out of the bed and went home. Later she married and had two children and seven grandchildren.

Now it was my turn to exercise the priesthood in behalf of the patient who had been my example, my father. I didn't know any eloquent language. After I had sealed the anointing, I just said, "I command you to be healed immediately and get up and go home." When I had said those words, my father got up, dressed, and went home. He had no problems with his heart for the rest of his life.

*The Lord God hath power to do all things
which are according to his word.*

Alma 7:8

The Last Obstacle

$\mathcal{F}$ or my wife and me, the road back to Church activity was long and hard. We had just reconciled and remarried after spending several agonizing years apart. Our divorce had not been the right answer. We had been miserable. Eventually we discovered that we really did love each other and we desperately wanted our children to be bound to us eternally. But qualifying for an eternal marriage now seemed a remote possibility.

During the years that we were divorced, we each had systematically defied the commandments and temple covenants. It was as though we had been trying as hard as we could to thumb our noses at God. In the process, we had managed to forfeit our memberships and lose the blessings of our former temple sealing. We had individually suffered through gut-wrenching legal issues, poverty, and absolute despair.

When we remarried and tried to piece our lives back together, my wife's health became a major concern. The years of stress had taken their toll in the forms of migraine headaches, fibromyalgia, and chronic fatigue. A possible cause, we thought, was her smoking. We both smoked. A lot. When we began to take the missionary lessons I was able to quit, but my wife could not. It broke her heart. We had faced the problems of our past one by one, resolved them with our bishop, and had moved forward. We had begun to pray individually and as a family. We had started to attend church, pay our tithing, and keep the commandments. We met with local and regional Church leaders to deal with every obstacle that stood between us and restoring our blessings.

But my wife's cigarette addiction still stood in the way. We would never make it unless she could overcome. She had tried all sorts of medical curatives, chewing gum, and mental disciplines. Nothing had worked.

Then, when all options had failed, she took her problem to God and was impressed to call our home teacher, who came to see us. He explained that addictions are more a spiritual than a physical ailment. He asked her about her commitment to Jesus Christ. Emotionally, she bore her testimony. He asked her if she believed that the Savior could heal her addiction. She answered yes. Then we knelt as a family in prayer and expressed our desire for the fullness of Church blessings. We pled that the Lord would deliver my wife from this most difficult and damaging addiction. When we concluded our prayer, our home teacher laid his hands upon my wife's head. He hadn't come in the name of science or medicine or even as a comforting counselor, he said; he had come in the name of the Lord. He commanded the cravings to cease and the addiction to depart.

She stood up beaming, a look of surprise on her face. She wasn't sure what she was feeling or what to think. The cravings were gone—immediately. She was free! She never smoked another cigarette, and shortly thereafter all of our blessings, including our temple sealing, were restored.

[God] has all power, all wisdom, and all understanding;
he comprehendeth all things, and he is a merciful Being,
even unto salvation, to those who will repent
and believe on his name.

ALMA 26:35

To Unstop the Ears of the Deaf

𝓝ew Zealand had been my son's mission. When my husband and I picked him up, the local members treated us like royalty. A couple escorted us around the island showing us the beauty of the place. We were invited to a special family home evening that was to be attended by a variety of members.

Arriving late was a man and his wife, who had a scarf tied about her head.

"She's not well," he told us. "It's her ear." He turned to my husband and said, "After dinner will you help me give her a blessing?"

"Of course," my husband answered.

The man seemed satisfied. He led his wife to a couch where she lay down and remained very still. When the hostess called us to dinner, the woman continued to lie quietly on the couch. We asked about her condition. She had been very sick for a month, we were told, and had hardly been able to eat during that time. Her hearing in one ear had been badly affected and she had experienced spells of deafness. We noticed that the ear appeared to be very sore; it was swollen from apparent internal pressure. Doctors—so-called—had been unable to determine the cause of her affliction or offer her relief.

When we had finished our dinner, we retired to the living room where the woman still lay on the couch. "Before we have the family home evening lesson," said her husband, "may we give my wife a blessing?"

He didn't wait for an answer. He produced a bottle of consecrated oil from his pocket and said to my husband, "I'll anoint and you give the blessing."

I saw my husband take a deep breath. He obviously had thought that the roles would be reversed. We had heard of the faith of the people of New Zealand. We knew that they placed great weight upon the power of the priesthood to heal.

My husband consented to the request, then added, "This is the first time we have met. I will be relying on the faith of you and your wife."

That said, the men laid their hands upon the head of the ailing woman and my husband, acting as voice, promised her in the name of the Lord an *immediate* healing. I looked up in surprise. It was uncharacteristic of him. I think the words surprised him too, but he spoke firmly and without hesitation.

When the blessing ended, the woman jumped up off the couch and ran into a bedroom. We all looked at each other perplexed. Her sister-in-law ran after her. After a few anxious moments, the sister-in-law returned and said, "She's all right. She's cleaning it up."

"Cleaning *what* up?" we asked.

"The infection. It has burst and is running out of her ear."

When the woman's ear had completely drained and she had "cleaned it up," she joined us and asked to eat dinner. She filled her plate to overflowing. For the remainder of the evening she participated fully in family home evening by singing, laughing, bearing testimony, and *listening* to the lesson. As she left, she grasped my husband's hands and said, "I'll never forget you."

"I'll never forget you, either," he replied.

And we never did forget each other. These many years we have continued to correspond and bask in a long-distance friendship that began long ago when the blessing of the Lord was sought and received.

"In my name they shall . . . unstop the ears of the deaf" (D&C 84:69).

The Lord is my rock, and my fortress, and my deliverer; my God, my strength, in whom I will trust; my buckler, and the horn of my salvation, and my high tower.

PSALM 18:2

Calming the Storms

When I was a boy, the Shreveport Louisiana Branch was large in comparison to the nearby Coushatta congregation, which was a "dependent branch." Coushatta's membership was so small that my father, who was president of both branches, often fulfilled every priesthood responsibility alone, including blessing and passing the sacrament. On Sundays, he would first conduct services at Shreveport and then he would drive to Coushatta and conduct services there.

The members of the Shreveport Branch were poor and persecuted. We held meetings in the Carpenters' Hall. Every Sunday morning, our family would arrive early and sweep up the cigarette butts and beer cans so that we would have a clean room in which to worship.

The accommodations for the Coushatta Branch were a step down. No one in that community would even rent a building to us, so we were forced to hold services in the woods. Dad made a pulpit of a tree stump and benches of split logs.

Louisiana is a rainy state. Frequently, as we held services in

Coushatta, the weather would turn foul. When storms threatened, my father would follow a simple pattern: He would interrupt the meeting; he and his one counselor would kneel to pray; and Dad would invoke the priesthood and plead with God to calm the elements.

I attended services in Coushatta for years and watched many storm clouds roil above our tiny gathering. I watched my father stop, kneel, and pray the storms away. Although it frequently rained around our Sunday services in Coushatta, it never rained on us.

❧

Believe in God; believe that he is, and that he created all things, both in heaven and in earth; believe that he has all wisdom, and all power, both in heaven and in earth.

MOSIAH 4:9

A Simple Prayer

I have heard people talk about miracle healings, but I have witnessed it only once. It came in response to a simple prayer, and it happened to me.

Early in our marriage, my husband took a job teaching school in a small Idaho community. I was able to stay at home and tend our one-year-old son. The flu had hit our town hard, and my baby was the first in the family to become ill. He needed my constant attention. I was a new mother and I didn't know much about caring for infants, especially when they were sick. He had a high fever and was vomiting. I did my best to make him comfortable.

One day, after my husband left for work, I felt myself becoming sick. The symptoms grew worse as the day progressed: aching muscles, dizziness, and nausea. I couldn't even stand without feeling sick to my stomach. I needed to be in bed. What could I do? I had no family nearby, and I didn't know my ward or neighbors yet. I didn't want to call my husband because he had just started his new job and getting a substitute teacher on such short notice was nearly impossible.

I knelt down and offered up an urgent prayer. I asked Heavenly Father for the impossible: to help me be well instantly. It was bold. I had never before asked for such a thing. I was sick, so my prayer was short and not very eloquent. But it was sincere. I truly needed help—now!

When I finished praying, I raised myself to my feet and found that the symptoms had vanished. I was well! I went back to work caring for my baby's needs and doing my daily chores. I felt absolutely normal, as if I had never been sick. I was astonished. Although I needed the blessing and had asked for it, I hadn't actually thought that it was possible.

❧

The Lord is the strength of my life;
of whom shall I be afraid?

PSALM 27:1

Burned!

Tragedy struck when my granddaughter Sasha was eighteen months old. Her insatiable curiosity had lured her to my sister Lynn's bedroom and the hot-water humidifier. Suddenly, we heard a ghastly scream and we sprinted to the bedroom. Sasha was holding up a hot, dripping wet sweater sleeve and a scalded hand and arm. Lynn and I grabbed her and headed for the cold-water tap. Sasha's mother was at work. I was tending. I had taken Sasha to visit my sister, Lynn, who has acute asthma and uses a humidifier to relieve the symptoms. Lynn was sure that she had turned off the humidifier that morning. Obviously not.

The child was screaming. As Lynn and I immersed Sasha's hand and arm in the cold water, I thought I would pass out from the sight. The skin on the hand was hanging in threads from the fingers. Slowly, we removed the sweater. The burn was worse than we had expected, if that were possible. It extended up the arm to the elbow, and the scalded flesh appeared to be melting off her arm and sliding down her blistered hand. I prayed for strength to remain calm and stay focused. I looked into my sister's face, which had gone pale. My heart was pounding hard. I began to pray to the Lord that we were doing the right thing and that Sasha's arm and hand could be saved.

We called Sasha's mother at work, then we called the emergency ward at the hospital to receive instructions and to alert them of the situation. I held Sasha, who buried her head in my neck and whimpered pitifully. She kept saying, "Hurts Gramma, hurts. I wuv you."

I tried to sound reassuring as we rushed to the hospital. "The doctor will make it better," I said, trying to console her. Over and over I repeated that she was my precious love. I needed to appear strong. I dared not show my emotions, but I felt as though I could break down at any moment. But whenever I glanced at the terrible burn, my heart broke; I was sobbing inside.

In a flurry of activity, the emergency room doctors went to work. From the outset, they seemed sober and not too optimistic. The arm was gruesome in appearance. The attending doctor informed us that all of the skin had to come off immediately. Sasha would not let go of me. The doctor had to work on her while I held her in my arms. I held out her burned arm as the doctor cut away the burned flesh and applied a dressing.

Now, Sasha's mother had arrived. I was so grateful that she had been spared the grisly sight. When Sasha saw her mother, she began to cry uncontrollably, and we all tried in vain to calm her. The child just wanted her mother to hold her and make the pain go away. None of us were keeping our emotional equilibrium at this point. No one knew how much damage had been done to the arm and hand; no one could tell us if she would be impaired for life. But we were about to find out. The next stop was a specialized burn center.

When the specialists unwrapped the wound to examine it, Sasha's mother got her first view of the burn. She immediately dropped down on a chair and her face turned the color of paste. A nurse practitioner rushed to her side and helped her put her head down between her legs. While my daughter was trying to recover, I took the attending doctor aside and asked him if Sasha would use the hand again. I was in for another shock. He said, "We'll have to worry about that later. Right now we need to see if we can save the arm."

I felt as though the floor would go out from under me. From that moment, the only thought in my mind was to get Sasha to the priesthood.

I called my home teacher and bishop to anoint and bless Sasha. From the moment the holy oil was placed on the child's head, a feeling of safety began to permeate us. We were suddenly filled with hope. What had been a dreadful day was now beginning to brighten. We began to relax and face the future with optimism. We knew that we were in for a long period of treatment and recovery, but we knew that a greater power had now taken charge of the situation and that all would be well. Finally, we were feeling at peace. What a blessing is the priesthood when all other options have been exhausted and life seems to be failing us at every turn.

The treatments were arduous. We learned to change Sasha's dressings three times daily. We drove her to the burn unit every other day. We had no idea how long this would go on. It didn't matter. We would do it for as long as was needed.

The procedures were painful. The burn had to be washed and the dead tissue had to be scraped or cut away. A skin graft was a future option, but the present goal was to save the arm and hand. But our efforts were paying off. A miracle was happening right before our eyes. Sasha's injury was healing rapidly. During our visits, the doctors at the burn center would regularly call in other doctors to look at the miraculous arm. They later confided to me that they had not expected that the arm could be saved.

Soon, the arm and hand began to take on a healthy pink hue. Sasha began to pick up objects and hold and play with them. This was remarkable considering the fact that her palm must have shed at least fourteen layers of dead skin. Once again, skin grafting was discussed, but the doctors held off. The healing process was proceeding nicely. The most seriously damaged area had been on the back of the hand and between the fingers. But now the tissues appeared to be miraculously reforming.

In time, all that remained of the burn was a small, tan-colored spot.

Our family is well aware that only through divine intervention were Sasha's arm and hand restored—without surgery or grafting! We did all we could, as did the doctors, and then we relied on the power of God to provide the ultimate healing. The arm and hand became beautiful, no scarring, no pigmentation problems—and they were totally functional! The doctors called it a miracle. Eighteen months later, when Sasha turned three, she was pronounced whole.

Only God could have done this.

❧

Thou reignest over all; and in thine hand is power and might; and in thine hand it is to make great, and to give strength unto all.

1 CHRONICLES 29:12

A Gift of Tongues

Spanish never came easily to me. I took two years of Spanish in junior high and one year in high school. Sadly, when the courses ended, I could only remember such phrases as "Hello, I am American. Do you speak English?" or "Your hair is pretty. Do you like my hair?" I never attempted to converse with anyone in Spanish because I was sure I would say something embarrassing.

I was called to serve a church service mission at Church headquarters in Salt Lake City and was assigned to help in the Family History department in the Joseph Smith Memorial Building. As a young 19-year-old service missionary, I became the designated grandson of the older missionaries, but I managed to avoid the cheek-pinching and hair-tussling. One of my duties was to assist patrons in preparing their genealogy with the Temple Ready® computer program, which formats ancestors' names so that temples can process them and make them ready for ordinance work.

One busy day, I was assisting some patrons with a computer problem. In the background, I heard some activity at the front desk. Interested, I walked over to see if I could help. A sister missionary asked if I knew anyone who spoke Spanish. A gentleman who did not speak a word of English was waving a computer disk, but no one could understand what he wanted to do with it.

I had absolutely zero confidence in my ability to speak Spanish, so I immediately began to search for a Spanish-speaking missionary. But I could find no one. I returned to the desk, where the man looked at me hopefully—so did the sister missionary. He fidgeted anxiously and kept glancing at the clock. He was obviously under some kind of time constraint. Then I felt a spiritual *push* that told me that I should do something for this man. I said a silent prayer, took an effectual step into the dark, and told the sister missionary that I knew a little Spanish from school. That's all she needed to hear. Suddenly I was elected!

As the man and I walked toward a computer, I desperately tried to recall every Spanish word I had ever learned. We sat down in front of a computer screen. He stared at me and I stared at him. Forcing a smile, I formed the words: *I don't know your language very well.* That broke the ice. He chuckled, patted me on the back, and proceeded to speak (in Spanish) very slowly about what he wanted to have done with the disk.

As he spoke, a most astonishing thing happened. Although I was unable to understand most of the words that he spoke, I was able to understand his meaning. It was as if a translator were standing between him and me. He talked about his deceased family, his parents, sisters, brothers, uncles, aunts, and cousins. And I understood! He wanted to prepare the names so that these people and others of his ancestors could receive their temple work. My feelings of inadequacy subsided as my understanding of his desires increased and, without conscious effort, I opened my mouth and began to answer his questions . . . in Spanish! Sometimes I made mistakes, but he kindly corrected me and taught me the proper phrase. The exchange between us was easy and natural!

I found that he and his family had come to Salt Lake City from South America for the sole purpose of doing this work. Their return flight was that night. I now understood why this man had seemed so insistent and anxious. As I hurried to submit his names to Temple Ready, we continued to converse in Spanish, easily, as if we were old friends.

Finally, when our task was completed, he graciously smiled, thanked me, and complimented me on my excellent Spanish. Only then was I struck with the full impact of what had occurred over the last few hours. The Spirit bore a strong witness to me that the Lord had allowed me to experience the gift of tongues to help this wonderful Spanish-speaking gentleman. As I stood at the front desk and watched him leave, I pondered the power of God that can provide such a miracle.

I have since tried to speak in Spanish but have found my skill limited to the few phrases that I could recall from junior high. The gift was gone. It was mine for a few precious hours and had served its purpose.

❧

Behold [God] is mightier than all the earth.

1 NEPHI 4:1

Knowledge of God

Before I formed thee in the belly I knew thee.

JEREMIAH 1:5

The Rusty Bucket of Rainwater

When I was a young child growing up in Monroe, Louisiana, Mother had a curious dream one Saturday night. She saw herself driving along a country road while my sister and I played in the back of the car. En route, my mother suddenly glanced in the rearview mirror and saw flames and smoke shooting from the trunk. Quickly she pulled to the side of the road, jumped out, and began searching for something to douse the flames. In a nearby gully, she spotted a rusty bucket filled with rainwater. She ran and grabbed it, hurried back to the car, and emptied the bucket on the fire. *A strange dream,* my mother thought as she awoke. And she let it go at that.

The next morning, Mother dressed us girls for church, and we piled into the car for the long drive to our little branch. About halfway there, on an infrequently traveled road, Mother was startled to see flames and smoke rising from the trunk of the car. My sister and I were frightened, but because of her dream Mother knew what to do. Pulling over to the side of the road, she quickly got out, ran about ten yards to a nearby gully, located a rusty bucket of rainwater, and returned and extinguished the fire. Then, catching her breath, she offered a simple prayer of gratitude, settled back in the car, and continued our drive to church.

✌

Known unto God are all his works
from the beginning of the world.

ACTS 15:18

Head-on Collision

 I n 1956, when my children were young, I used to drive extensively
in and around Ohio on various Church assignments. At one point, a
haunting thought began to obsess me: *What would I do if I were ever
faced with a head-on collision?* I reflected on the question over and
over again. An answer began to form in my mind.

"The impact of smashing into the steering wheel would surely
kill me," I would say to myself, "so I would only have a split second
to react and throw myself clear."

Thereafter, whenever the warning would return to my mind, I
would practice *saving myself* as I drove. The exercise went like this: First,
I would pick a distant spot on the road where I imagined the collision
might occur; then, as I approached it, at the last possible moment, I
would imagine throwing myself down to my right on the seat.

The unsettling thought tormented me for about a year, and each
time it entered my mind I would repeat the life-saving exercise. I
must have practiced it hundreds of times.

One night in September, I was scheduled to drive to a Church
meeting in Mansfield, Ohio. After dinner, I asked my wife if she and

the children would like to accompany me. She agreed, so we loaded our three kids in the car and started on our journey. At dusk, about twelve miles from our destination, we entered a narrow two-lane bridge. Suddenly, I saw a car speeding crazily toward us—on the wrong side of the road! I knew that a collision was unavoidable. The two cars slammed into each other at the middle of the bridge. My wife was holding our six-month-old son on her lap. The baby's head went through the windshield and shards of glass were sticking out of his face, one near his eye. My wife suffered two fractured bones in a forearm. Our other two children were lying on the backseat. Our oldest son suffered a severe whiplash and a ruptured spleen. Our daughter received a compound fracture to her skull.

I was the only one who was not injured. When I regained my senses, I found myself safely lying on the right seat, clear of the steering wheel, which would have crushed me. I had been warned months in advance, and I had been coached what to do. Beyond the miracle of my life being spared, there was another miracle. My family now needed a full-time caregiver. As the only one not injured, I was able to assume that responsibility.

The warning was obviously for one time and place. To this day, almost forty years later, I have never had that specific thought of warning return to my mind.

◆

The Lord knoweth all things which are to come.

WORDS OF MORMON 1:7

In a Flicker of Time

My husband is an avid racquetball player and was practicing daily to compete in an upcoming state championship tournament. He came home early one day after a strenuous workout complaining of a terrible headache. He took a strong pain pill and went to bed. I knew from past experience that the medication would knock him out for four or five hours.

However, about an hour later I heard him calling my name. His voice was filled with anxiety, and I hurried to see what the problem was. He was groggy from the pain pill, but with great animation he said to me, "Find the boys. Something is wrong!"

I hesitated. Then I said, "I'm sure they're okay. They're just playing out in the yard."

"Hurry!" he said with urgency.

I quickly ran from the room to find our boys. I could not see them anywhere. I circled the house twice. I checked everywhere. I was becoming quite alarmed when I heard their voices. At first I couldn't determine where they were but soon discovered they were in the garage. They were lying on the floor with their legs sticking out from under our station wagon. Relieved, I called them out from under the car and asked what they had been doing. They said, "We've been trying to light our leftover firecrackers, but the wind keeps blowing out our matches. So we were trying to light the matches under the car."

I felt my heart begin to pound. The spot that they had chosen to light their fireworks was right underneath the gas tank. It had been leaking small amounts of gasoline for several days!

Those two boys got the hug of their life—from sheer relief! Then they got a stern lecture! Afterward, we went to find Dad and give thanks to God.

❧

*Your Father knoweth what things ye
have need of, before ye ask him.*

MATTHEW 6:8

The Lord's Lost-and-Found Department

I teach seminary. In order to complete a project before class started, I awoke at 4:15 A.M. with the intention of heading to the seminary building early. As I walked past the dresser, I discovered that my keys to the building were not there. I searched all the logical places. Then I searched the less likely ones, but without success. I dared not call another teacher at this hour to borrow his keys.

I suddenly realized that there was only one thing to do. I knelt and explained my need to my Father in Heaven. A question came into my mind: "How can I let the Lord know that I have faith that he will help me find the keys?"

I got up from my knees, showered, shaved, dressed in my suit, and filled my briefcase. I had prepared in every way I could to receive the answer I needed. Then I knelt down again.

Just as I began my prayer, I remembered something. I saw myself the night before, running across the backyard in the darkness. I had stepped in a hole and had fallen to the ground.

"Thank you, Father," I said. Then I stood, walked out into the backyard, and picked up the keys from where they had slipped from my pocket.

As I drove to work that morning, I was grateful to my mom who had taught me as a young boy how to access the Lord's Lost-and-Found Department, and I remembered another time I had needed the Lord's help to locate something. I remembered staring into the white froth of a river as water tumbled over the rocks and debris and raced under a bridge. Tears gathered in the corners of my eyes and slid down my face and into the torrent below. I had been looking down into the river, and suddenly my glasses were gone! Now I stared through amblyopia and myopia into the plunging swirl, but there was nothing. I scrambled down the bank and into the water, bending, reaching, feeling, bracing my nine-year-old body against the current. The churning water made it impossible to see anything. My blind groping was useless. The glasses were gone!

Finally I climbed out of the water and stood on the bank gathering courage to go home and tell my parents that my carelessness would once again cost them money. Forty minutes later, Mother and I stood together where I had stood alone. "Did you see where they fell?" she asked.

I pointed at a spot with stones and sticks and a white whirlpool of water. I was sobbing now, surrendering to my emotions. I hated to be in trouble; I was in trouble a lot. I hated to lose things; I lost things all the time. Dad worked so hard to support his family. Our budget wasn't built to withstand my constant assaults.

"Did you pray?" Mother asked.

I had not. I knew the words and the formalities of prayer; I said them regularly, but I did not expect answers.

"Come on," she said. "Hold my hand. Will you ask Heavenly Father to help us?"

I took her hand and looked at her. Her eyes were already closed, and in my heart a quiet voice whispered, "She gets answers." I felt something small and warm moving in me, drying up the sadness. I bowed my head and squeezed my eyes shut.

"Heavenly Father, I lost my glasses. Daddy can't afford new ones and I need 'em to see good and do better in school. Will you please help us find them? Name of Jesus, amen."

Mom gave me a pat on the bottom, and I climbed down the bank again and waded into the water to the spot where the glasses had disappeared. I plunged in my hand and grasped a handful of sticks. After a moment's hesitation, I drew them from the water and examined them. My glasses were there! They had been caught by the temple piece among the twigs and rubble.

The small, warm thing in me grew then, as I stood in the water. It grew and became a shining certainty: "God hears; God answers."

❧

The eyes of the Lord are in every place.

PROVERBS 15:3

In an Instant

I had been working night and day to prepare a proposal for my employer. I was supposed to present it later that afternoon. Typing was not my talent, nor would it ever be. Oh where was my secretary? I was exhausted. I slowly pounded out the words, but I was becoming more frustrated by the moment.

Suddenly my office began to spin and sickening dizziness overcame me. I grabbed my head as though I could stop the vertigo and achieve a sense of balance, but it did no good. I needed to lie down, but not here. Gingerly, I made my way out of the building and to my car. Somehow I managed to drive home and crawl into bed.

Then things got worse.

For much of my life, I have suffered with an inner ear problem that is aggravated by stress. When I have an attack, the effects can last for days. The last time this had happened I had lain in bed for ten days until my head stopped spinning.

My daughter found me midday, lying in bed. She immediately understood the implications of my missing that very important meeting at work. But I could do nothing. I dared not move. I was feeling more and more sick. All I could tell her to do was leave the room and shut the door. By now I was clammy and sweating profusely. I thought, *Of all the days that this would happen, why today? If my job is not on the line it is surely in question. People have flown in from 2,000 miles away to hear my proposal . . . and I can't even move!*

I said a prayer. I have always believed in prayer, but I have rarely experienced a prayer that was answered on my schedule. Nevertheless I prayed. I lay on the bed, held my head in a fixed position, closed my eyes, and prayed hard.

About fifteen minutes passed, then I heard the phone ring. In the next room, I heard my daughter answer it and say, "Yes, Mother is here but she is unable to come to the phone. . . . Oh no, no, she would not want you to come here, not now."

Good for her, I thought. *The last thing I need is a visitor.* My hair was a sweaty, matted fright, and I had washed my face clean of makeup. To top it off, I was wearing only a ratty old robe. I didn't want anybody to see me, and for sure I was not moving off that bed!

The whirling room had begun to make me feel sick to my stomach. A pounding noise was coming from my spinning head. Or at least that is what I thought. As I trained my ear, I realized that the pounding was coming from the front door. My daughter answered. I heard the familiar voice of my friend who had phoned only minutes earlier. He had come to the house! My son had now joined my daughter and they were saying, "No, you can't see her. Mom is too sick to see anyone." Then their voices hushed, and I could not hear what was being said. No matter what, I was not going to move. If I did, I would be making a fast trip to the bathroom!

Suddenly, my daughter stuck her head in my room. She said, "Mom, you have to come into the living room right now."

"Are you crazy?" I grumbled. "I'm as sick as a dog!"

"But Mom, you have to."

My daughter came and pulled at my arm. I protested but slowly came to a sitting position. Then I carefully stood. The room rolled. I leaned up against the wall and held onto the doorframe. My daughter urged me forward, and I shuffled into the living room, protesting and growling all the way.

There, in the middle of the room—and to my embarrassment—was my good friend. He looked sheepishly at me and stepped forward to assist me into a chair. I squeezed my eyes closed. If I couldn't see how awful I looked, neither might he.

"What on earth are you doing here?" I asked. My son and daughter were sitting close by me. We waited for an answer.

My friend began to explain, "I was driving home when suddenly your name came into my mind. I felt a prompting that you needed help. I felt a great sense of urgency. I stopped the car and found a phone to call you. Then I drove straight over."

By now I was doubled over in my chair holding my aching, spinning head. I was too sick to respond. He continued by saying, "I have come to give you a priesthood blessing. Is that all right with you?"

I whispered, "Yes."

He then addressed my children and asked if they believed the holy priesthood to be the power of Jesus Christ to heal.

They answered, yes.

He stepped behind me and placed his hands on my head. From

past priesthood blessings I expected a long prayer, loving words of comfort, and a request that the Lord might help me feel better. But this is what happened: With a strong, resounding voice and without the least hesitation, he stated the power of the priesthood and in the name of Jesus Christ he commanded the sickness to leave my body . . . immediately!

And immediately, I felt something like a glove sliding off my body. It started from my head, fell off my shoulders and arms, over my torso, around my back, down my legs, and out of my feet. I collapsed into a sobbing heap. For the moment I was unable to speak. I dared not move or open my eyes. Scared, my daughter ran to me and asked if I was all right. I composed myself, straightened, and looked up at her. I had felt the sickness leave me as though it had been a tangible object. It had lost its grip, and something had ripped it from my system. I had felt as if the sickness had passed through my body, exited through the bottoms of my feet, and spilled out onto the floor.

Within a few seconds I was able to stand and shake the hand of my friend. We all had tears in our eyes. I thanked him. I walked him to the door and bid him goodbye. Then I went to shower and dress. Within the hour I was back at work with no dizziness or sickness. I met the people who had traveled the long distance and I gave them a fine presentation.

❧

The Lord is a God of knowledge,
and by him actions are weighed.

1 SAMUEL 2:3

To Listen Carefully

I was running late, hurrying to get everything into the station wagon. I was in charge of a church play and needed to get the costumes to rehearsal on time. Tomorrow was opening night. To complicate matters, I would have to take the baby with me since no one was home to tend him.

In those days, almost thirty years ago, seatbelts were mainly used in airplanes. Traveling in cars without them was the norm. I had purchased a car bed for the baby that fastened over the back of the front seats with two hooks. It would have to do today. I was late!

Hurrying out to the station wagon, I fitted the car bed in place and arranged the baby's bedding. Then I went back into the house and fetched him. I checked my watch. Late, late, late! To drive the round trip would take three hours. I needed to get going! The freeways were always crowded at this time of the day and I had wanted to give myself plenty of time to pick up the costumes and get to the church building on time. But I was late!

As I walked toward the car with the baby, I suddenly had the strangest feeling not to go. Forget the trip! I tried to dismiss the thought, imagining the implications, but the feeling persisted. I looked into the face of my three-month-old child and he gave me a big smile. So dear and precious. Again I felt something like a voice telling me not to go. My baby began to squirm and wanted to play. I cooed at him and continued toward the car. I shook off the feeling and placed him in the car bed, his feet behind my back and his head behind the passenger's seat. As I drove I would be able to turn and see him. Nice for Mommy.

I started the car and then the feeling came again. This time the feeling said that I should leave my baby at home. What was I to do? Our neighbors were elderly, not the babysitting type. My husband was at work. The older children were at school. Now I was *really* late!

I said a quick prayer. "Please, I need help!"

I got back into the car and turned on the motor. Just then my husband drove up.

Puzzled, I asked, "Why are you home?"

"I decided to come home for lunch."

I told him about the three-hour trip that I needed to make and asked him if he could cancel his appointments for several hours to stay home with the baby. He agreed. I lifted the baby out of the car bed, handed him to his father.

As I was driving down the freeway at 70 miles per hour, I suddenly saw a car in front of me begin to swerve sideways. Obviously in trouble, it turned onto the shoulder of the freeway. The next car lurched in the opposite direction. Quickly, the freeway was a mass of red brake lights. Cars were skidding and veering crazily in every lane. Instinctively, I slammed on my brakes to avoid broadsiding the automobile in front of me. As I did, the baby's car bed flew past me and smashed into the windshield.

My heart was beating so fast I could barely think. It took a few moments for me to realize that if my beautiful son had been in the car bed, his little body would have been thrown into the windshield at 70 miles per hour.

I was so grateful for the warning. After these many years, I am still grateful. Since then, I have tried to listen carefully to the voice. It has never steered me wrong.

❧

Remember the former things of old: for I am God, and there is none else; I am God, and there is none like me, declaring the end from the beginning, and from ancient times the things that are not yet done, saying, My counsel shall , stand and I will do all my pleasure.

Isaiah 46:9–10

Fifty Dollars

Sometimes we find ourselves in a free fall not of our own choosing; at other times we choose the free fall, trusting that God will catch us. We chose the latter and were not disappointed.

When my wife and I were courting, we often talked about trusting the Lord. We were students and poor, and we had agreed to not postpone having children. Finances, we knew, would be challenging.

"Sweetheart," I asked her one Sunday morning, "what will we do if the time comes when we simply do not have enough to get by?"

"We'll trust the Lord," she said.

"How will we demonstrate that kind of trust?"

"What does your mother do when she is in financial difficulty? Does she pay less tithes and offerings?"

"No, she pays more."

"We'll do something like that," she said. "We'll take whatever we have, donate it to the Lord, tell him our needs, and trust him."

Two years went by. We had a baby and another was on the way. Medical bills and car repairs had left us with fourteen dollars in the bank. We needed fifty. The next paycheck was a week and a half away.

We sat at the kitchen table talking on Saturday afternoon. "Do you remember what we decided when we were dating?" my wife asked me.

I remembered. But that was talk. We were down to our last fourteen dollars with no prospect of more for ten days.

"We made a covenant," she continued. "The Lord has never let us down, and he won't now."

The next morning we gave an offering of fourteen dollars to the bishop. Then we knelt and told the Lord we needed fifty and that we trusted him.

As we returned to our apartment after church, the phone was ringing. It was my mother. We visited for a moment, then she asked, "Do you remember in elementary school when you used to take a quarter to school each week and buy U.S. Savings Bonds?"

I had a vague recollection. It had been a long time.

"I was in the basement this morning," she continued, "and I opened an old box. I saw an envelope with two bonds that you bought in 1954 and 1955."

"What denomination are they?" I asked. A small, warm thing began to stir within me.

"They are $25-dollar bonds," she said. "They are past maturity, so they must be worth a little more than fifty dollars."

Did the Lord know when I was in the second grade that one day my wife and I would need fifty dollars? Of course he did.

❧

[God] hath determined the times before appointed.

ACTS 17:26

Twice Protected

My parents said they would not support me if I chose to serve a mission. If I wanted it that badly, they said, I'd better earn the money myself. I wanted a mission, so I took a summer job in Alaska, where I would work in the kitchen of a lodge.

The staff worked long hours all week long. We had no televisions or phones. The national park at Glacier Bay was on a peninsula, so we had few places to see. But we saw the kitchen—a lot! *It will be worth it,* I thought. *At the end of the summer I will have earned enough for my mission.*

I was wrong. I had no way of knowing at the time that the owners of the lodge were in financial trouble, and they were saying nothing about their situation to their employees.

Soon after I arrived, I fell in love with one of the waitresses. She was beautiful and fun, and I found that I was talking myself out of a mission when I was around her. But I wanted to do what was right. I took my concern to Heavenly Father. He would know whether I should get married or serve a mission. Either way, I expected that I would have enough money.

I prayed all one night. Early in the morning, I received a distinct impression that I would soon be taken from this place and from the girl and that I would serve a mission. I was too tired to be shocked. I had asked for an answer, and I knew that I must follow the counsel of God. I looked at the clock. 5:30 A.M. I got up off my knees and showered and dressed for work.

Later, after the workday had ended, the staff decided to have some diversion. We played basketball and jumped on a trampoline. Feeling quite macho and wanting to show off a bit, I attempted a somersault. But I was unable to tuck and I fell awkwardly on the back on my neck. The impact knocked the air out of me, and I felt a sudden, terrible pain in my neck. Concerned, my friends helped me back to my room, where I climbed into the top bunk and tried to rest. But the throbbing grew worse. I had never experienced such pain.

As I lay in bed for the next six days, I prayed for relief. I could not move; I could not sleep; I could not work. I could do nothing except try to endure the agonizing pain. My friends tried homemade remedies such as pouring lemon liniment on my back and neck. One friend gave me a massage.

Frustrated with bed rest, I decided that I would endure the pain and get back to work. I held my head absolutely still and walked the half-mile from my bunkhouse to the kitchen, but once I arrived, my boss took one look at me and sent me back to bed.

Now my friends were becoming more worried. We all began to suspect that this was more than a temporary whiplash. Doctors were scarce in that part of Alaska, but a retired doctor lived thirteen miles away. My friends laid me in the back of a pickup and drove me the distance on rutted roads. When the old doctor had examined me, he said that there was nothing he could do. I would need to be life-flighted to a hospital in Juneau for X rays. The doctor made me a makeshift neck brace, and my friends rigged a bed in the twin prop plane.

The air was turbulent. As I was jostled from side to side, the pain in my neck increased. Once we landed and I felt the firm earth once more beneath my feet, I felt an element of relief, but the pain was still intense. After four hours of X rays, the doctors discovered that my neck had been badly broken. I was not prepared for the news. To make matters worse, they said that there was nothing they could do to help except place me in traction to keep me immobile and give me morphine to ease the pain.

I began to panic. I was far from home and all alone. I called the mission president and another priesthood holder to come to the hospital and administer to me. Although they did not know me, they responded to the call and came immediately. When they entered the room, I experienced a feeling of relief. The mission president then laid his hands on my head and began to offer a blessing of healing. I felt a warmth flow into me. Then came the promises: I would be healed and I would be able to serve a mission. All would be well!

One week later, I was flown to Seattle to a special orthopedic hospital. There, I once again endured hours of X rays and tests. The doctors emerged from their consultation shaking their heads. They said that only a miracle had prevented me from being quadriplegic. When I had fallen, I had crushed and separated six of the seven vertebrae at the C-7th cervix of my neck. In some amazing way, one small bone chip had wedged to keep the seventh vertebra from severing. Otherwise, I would have had no use of my arms or legs for the rest of my life. The specialists fitted me with a full body cast and released me to my parents' care. In six weeks, I was scheduled to receive a neck fusion operation in Seattle.

I never knew such depression as I experienced during that period of time. Satan's buffeting was relentless and merciless. I dismissed the promises that I had been given in the blessing in Alaska. I certainly had been taken away from my employment and the girl, but in what condition? And what about being able to serve a mission? The idea seemed preposterous in my present condition. At my lowest point, when I had lost all hope, I offered a prayer for deliverance, and it was during this prayer that I heard the words, "Your parents are to take you to the McKay-Dee Hospital in Ogden, Utah, where the doctors will examine you."

Suddenly emboldened, the depression abruptly lifted from my mind, I called for my parents to tell them what I had learned from prayer. Being less active in the Church and having opposed my mission, they certainly were not of a mind to accept what I knew to be an answer to my prayers. Receiving spiritual information through prayer and priesthood blessings was foreign to them then. They strongly disagreed with me. They reminded me that my fusion operation was scheduled for the next week in Seattle. But I was insistent, and they finally relented.

The night that I checked into the McKay-Dee Hospital was one of the most frightening and depressing of my life. I felt such thick darkness in my room that I did not dare close my eyes for fear that my life would be taken. I called upon the Lord for protection and waited anxiously for the first light of morning.

When the doctor arrived, he instructed the attendants to cut off my body cast and take me to X ray. Then came the confirmation of a miracle. After a complete examination, he said, "Your neck has completely healed. It is stronger than before you broke it. This can only be explained as a gift from God."

After eight long weeks of intense trial, I had gained an understanding of God's love for me. That fact changed my life forever. I walked out of the hospital with absolutely nothing wrong with me. Just as God had foreseen and told me, I would be leaving Alaska and not getting married. He wanted me to serve a mission.

I was never paid for my work in Alaska. Upon the doctor's pronouncing me whole, I took two full-time jobs, which I worked for five months night and day until the time that I departed for my mission. I was able to save barely enough, but it was sufficient to support me for two years. The entire experience became the foundation of my testimony. I came to understand that God knows, loves, and protects his children, and that he will guide and provide for us if we will trust him.

❧

Great is our Lord, and of great power:
his understanding is infinite.
PSALM 147:5

One Cab in 20,000

We received word that our son had become seriously ill while serving a mission in the Philippines. Once a strong, healthy 180-pound young man, he had now dropped to 140 pounds and was so sick that he could hardly get out of bed. Immediately we were given permission to travel and see him. We would take him home when he was well enough to board a plane.

We are not a wealthy family. Each month we scraped together enough to pay the costs of our son's mission. Now, learning that he had been hospitalized, we emptied the savings account, applied for passports and bought tickets, and made the trip. All that mattered was our son.

When we arrived in Manila, we hailed a taxi and headed for the hospital. With so much on my mind, I didn't even attempt to communicate with the cab driver, but my husband tried to strike up a conversation. The man didn't seem to understand English. My husband was trying to explain that our son was a Mormon missionary and was quite sick. That was why we needed to rush to the hospital. The taxi driver didn't respond.

When we arrived at the hospital, we paid the driver and he sped away. Then we headed for the hospital entrance. Suddenly I stopped.

My heart began to pound. I had left my bag in the cab! It contained all our money, charge cards, passports, and airline tickets.

Trying to achieve a sense of hope I said to my husband, "Maybe the driver will notice my bag and be honest enough to return to the hospital, find me, and give it back." But when the words spilled from my mouth they sounded more desperate than realistic. We were in a very poor country where cab drivers often work fifteen hours shifts and bring home two dollars a day. The money that my purse contained would seem like a fortune to him.

I was sick inside. In the blink of an eye and momentarily distracted, I had lost everything that we needed to cover our expenses in the Philippines and be able to return home. Everything was gone, and I knew it. I had never felt so frightened.

I told my husband to go into the hospital to be with our son while I flagged down cab drivers to ask for help. He relented. We both knew that our son needed a parent with him. As my husband entered the hospital, I began to madly hail every cab that passed. It was all I could think to do.

My task seemed impossible from the beginning. There are over 20,000 cabs in the city of Manila. Walking up and down the streets, I prayed and prayed that Heavenly Father would help me find the cab that contained my bag. I knew that God knew where the bag was, and I knew that only God knew how to get it back to me.

It was dark now. We had been searching for most of the day. When we stepped into our hotel room, my husband headed for the bed and collapsed. I left him to rest and went to find a pay phone to call our family back home.

Then, just as I stepped out of the hotel, I spotted the cab driver parked across the street. Wildly, I began to wave my arms. As I started to rush toward him, the doorman of the hotel stopped me. He pointed to a small woman. She was the driver's wife. She had just arrived at the hotel and was asking for me. Who can know the gratitude I felt when this humble, honest Filipino woman walked up to me and handed me my bag. She said her husband didn't know much English, but he had understood that our son was a Mormon missionary and was sick in the hospital. Together, they had realized that the money and papers in my bag were for our expenses and our return trip. They had searched the bag in order to find a clue to find us. They found a scrap of paper on which I had jotted down the name of our hotel. They came right away.

When we parted she hugged me. I could not hide my emotions. Heavenly Father had in fact known where my bag was all along, and he did know how to safely return it to us. He had touched the hearts of honest and gracious people.

I was amazed at their integrity. In their impoverished condition, the money would have helped their family enormously. I continue to be in awe. I have often wondered what might have happened if God had allowed us to hail some other of the 20,000 cabs in Manila.

❧

The Lord searcheth all hearts, and understandeth all the imaginations of the thoughts: if thou seek him, he will be found of thee.

1 CHRONICLES 28:9

Ask, Fast, and Go

Some places in missions are affectionately called "holes." That was what other missionaries had called the city that was to be my new assignment. But when I arrived and met the president and a newly formed branch, my feelings began to change. Although his branch was young and struggling, this man of faith seemed undeterred. He expected miracles and set out to obtain them.

My companion and I attended the branch's first correlation meeting. At the top of the list of the president's concerns was the absence of young men and women in the branch. Heavenly Father knew where to find these young people, the branch president said—and the president knew what to do. We all knelt to pray. We would begin to fast to find young people for our branch, and my companion and I would go to work.

Shortly thereafter, a young woman asked a member about the Church, and the member promptly invited her to attend our meetings on Sunday. The young woman came, and she brought five friends with her! We made appointments to visit them and their families. Less than three weeks later, eight young women and men were baptized and became the foundation of our youth program.

In our next correlation meeting, the branch president discussed the need for more priesthood holders. He prayed and presented our concern to the Lord. We all began to fast, and my companion and I went to work. The Lord knew where priesthood holders could be found, the president said. We just had to go find them.

Shortly thereafter, some members decided to introduce a few of their friends to the gospel. Some of those friends just happened to be men. Later that month two fine men were baptized into the Church, greatly strengthening the priesthood foundation of the branch.

During our next correlation meeting the Relief Society said they needed more members. The branch president again set the example by asking the Lord for help. We all agreed to fast for this special blessing, and my companion and I went searching. This time the Lord gave us more than we had asked for—he led us to an entire family to teach. The mother of the family was a welcome blessing to the branch's fledgling Relief Society. The father added to the ranks of the priesthood, and the children made the branch come alive.

This young branch president set an example of faith. He understood the most basic of gospel principles: Ask God for help; fast in faith; then go and do all you can. Within a few months of my arrival, the branch's numbers had tripled. It was truly a miracle.

❧

There is no God beside me, and all things are
present with me, for I know them all.

MOSES 1:6

Tornado

Many families in our Mississippi ward get together on Monday nights to hold joint family home evenings. We had gathered at a member's home and were having our lesson when a terrible storm began. Soon sirens screamed warnings. We knew what that meant. A violent F-2 tornado was raging through Lincoln County. We hunkered down, as we had been taught, and waited for the storm to pass.

The tornado cut a devastating path through our community. Trees twisted in the whirlwind; some broke in half and others were uprooted. Power poles snapped like twigs, and many mobile homes blew over. Some residents were injured or trapped in their homes. High winds from the tornado damaged a church, and forested land was leveled. At least five homes of the LDS members in our group were damaged or destroyed, but the families were safe. They had been somewhere else, holding family home evening.

After the storm passed, we emerged to assess the damage. The area looked like a war zone. The entire community—LDS members, Baptists, Methodists, and others—worked together to help each other. We cleared roads and driveways, and we cut down broken trees or lifted them off houses, but for many days, the more we cleaned up, the worse it looked. Because of the damage, it was two weeks before I was able to return to my home. I am convinced that the Lord protected us from the storm. He knew where we were and where we needed to be that night. He knew where the tornado would touch down and how to steer us clear. For years the prophets have told us that holding family home evening will protect our families from the storms of life. But I had never thought about the storms of nature.

❧

My name is Jehovah, and I know the end from the beginning; therefore my hand shall be over thee.

ABRAHAM 2:8

Cut the Rope!

My friends and I loved to ride horses in the canyons near Brigham Young University. We had scheduled to go riding the next day. The night before our ride, I had a dream that one of the horses hated to have its head tied. As it was being tethered, it reared up, fell down, and began to strangle by its own weight pulling against the harness rope. I dreamed that we rushed forward in order to cut the rope and save the horse, but the young man who owned the horses shouted, "No, it's a new rope!" We hesitated and tried to find a way to salvage the rope. As a result, the horse was badly injured.

The next morning, as we drove to Payson Canyon to ride, I related this dream to my friends. While we were saddling up, the owner of the horses told us that one of the mares hated to have her head tied. I immediately noticed that her halter rope had been improperly fastened so that it could not come undone in an emergency. As I reached out to fix it, the horse threw back her head, obviously frightened that she was going to be tethered, and began to fight against the rope. She reared up wildly then came down hard on a post and fell to her side. Suddenly, the halter and halter rope were strangling her.

"Cut the rope!" someone yelled.

"No!" cried the owner. "It's a new rope!"

Everyone froze in disbelief, having just heard me relate the details of my strange dream. We knew what to do. We quickly rushed forward and slashed the rope. The horse lay there shaking and sweating for a few minutes but was soon was able to stand on its feet. The mare suffered no injury because I had been forewarned, and I knew that we must not hesitate to cut the new rope.

❧

God know[s] all things, being from everlasting to everlasting.
MORONI 7:22

Don't Plan Anything

God is perfectly capable of presenting us with a solution to our challenges. He knows when to tell us to speed up, slow down, turn to the right or to the left—or just to do nothing.

My husband is in the United States Army. About a month after we were married, he received orders for an "unaccompanied" tour of duty in South Korea. His assignment was to be one full year. I knew what that meant: The army would not pay for me to go with him or cover our living expenses or medical benefits. The prospect of his being gone that long was more than I could bear.

I expressed my anxiety to the Lord and asked for help. The subject became a central theme of my daily prayers. Then I began to do all I could to come up with an answer. I had heard of spouses going to Korea and getting jobs as English teachers, so I decided to check it out. But something strange happened. Every time I began to research teaching in Korea or whenever I asked someone about it, I had the feeling I shouldn't be obsessed with trying to find an opportunity: "Don't worry about it. Don't plan anything. Something will work out. Have faith."

I speculated that maybe I wasn't supposed to go to Korea; perhaps I was supposed to go home and live with my parents for a year. But I felt the same way about moving home: "Don't worry about it. Don't plan anything. Something will work out. Have faith."

As the time grew closer for my husband to leave, I found myself more anxious about trying to plan for the year. But each time I tried to force an answer, I felt the same impression: "Don't be concerned." I wanted to say, "But are you watching the calendar?!"

One day the impression changed, and I felt that my husband and I should pack up all our belongings and go to visit my parents. After a short visit, my husband would have to leave for Korea. We packed up and traveled to my parents' home. I still had no idea what I was going to do for the next year or where I was going to live. But the feeling persisted: "Don't worry about it. Don't plan anything. Something will work out. Have faith."

Then something remarkable happened. A week before my husband was scheduled to leave, my sister came home from high school one day with a newspaper clipping. She said it was really strange because she usually didn't read the newspaper, and she never looked through the classified ads. But one of her teachers had given the class an assignment to survey the newspaper. My sister's attention had been drawn to a small advertisement for an English teacher in South Korea. There was a phone number.

I had a strong feeling that I should call. Soon I was talking to the director of a school in Korea.

The school was looking to hire a college graduate to teach English to its students. I had a Bachelor of Science degree.

The school would need someone for just one year. My husband would be stationed in Korea for a year.

They would pay my airfare to Korea and back home after one year. They would provide an apartment to live in, good pay, medical benefits, vacation time, sick leave, and bonuses!

They needed someone immediately. I was already packed!

After I had spoken with the director and some of the American teachers who worked there, I received the confirming feeling that I was supposed to go to Korea and take this job!

The director offered me the job over the phone and I accepted. I arrived in Korea two weeks later, just as my husband was scheduled to begin his assignment.

The incredible blessings that I received during my year teaching English in Korea are innumerable. I will always be grateful that I trusted the Lord and followed his promptings. I know that if we listen, he will guide us.

God knoweth all the times which are
appointed unto man.
ALMA 40:10

Love of God

God is love.

1 JOHN 4:8

For the First Time, I Saw a Bird

I was born with only partial vision—a condition that isn't correctable. But I have never let my disability stop me from enjoying life. I am married; I have six beautiful children; I acquired a college education; and I have participated in many events that others would have thought impossible. However, I have never gotten over wanting to enjoy normal vision and to be able to more fully enjoy the world. I have dreamed about how seeing clearly would change my life and how amazing it would be.

Some of God's creations that I have especially wished to enjoy are beautiful birds. I have seen them on television, in movies, and in books, but I have seen very little of their beauty in real life. I can perceive their figures moving from one tree to another, but they appear only as small black objects against the bright backdrop of the sky. I hear their beautiful music, but I have been unable to discern in any detail their color and grace.

One autumn, our family had the opportunity to go to Rainier National Park in the state of Washington. The leaves were colorful, the air was crisp and clear, the sun was bright, and the park was virtually deserted. When we stopped for a rest, my wife took our children to the restroom, and I sat down on a picnic bench. Once again I heard what I could not see: birds singing in the tall pines. I looked up and saw the small black objects flitting from tree to tree. Wishing I could see their beauty, I prayed, "Please heal my vision and allow me to see these glorious creations."

What happened next was a miracle. As I was saying the words of my prayer, a beautiful bird landed on my hand directly in front of my face. It was not more than six inches away, exactly where my vision was best. For the first time in my life I could see a bird! It looked at me and I looked at it. The bird turned around and let me enjoy its full loveliness. I thanked God for this opportunity, and as I did many more birds of all varieties landed on my table. Then I prayed that I might share this experience with my family. As they returned, they saw what was happening and sat down quietly at the table. The birds were not frightened, but remained. We played with the birds until it was time to leave.

I can still see the details of the birds in my mind. It was an experience that is burned into my memory. I will always thank God for hearing my prayer and allowing me to enjoy a great outpouring of his love.

❧

I am encircled about eternally in the arms of his love.

2 NEPHI 1:15

No Food in the House

*D*uring a particularly difficult financial time, I turned to God for help. I suppose that I am like other people whose prayers are offered with more feeling in times of urgent need. I remember feeling ashamed that I had not previously put more effort into my relationship with God when money had been plentiful. Still, believing that such petitioning could help, I arose one morning and began to plead for help.

The answer came in a strange way. A thought entered my mind: *Your friend Paul [name changed] has no food in his house. Go and take him some money.*

"But I have so little," I said aloud. Then, considering to whom I was talking, I asked, "How much?"

One hundred dollars.

I felt anxiety shoot through me. One hundred dollars was all I had in the bank! I searched myself, hoping that I had imagined the whole thing. I tried to pray again but felt only silence. Then, through the quiet I perceived a message. It seemed to say, *Will you trust me or not?*

Paul was a good man who had recently lost his income source and was struggling through very difficult financial times. No effort of his had seemed to be able to stop the rapid decline of his assets and reserves.

I drove to the bank, withdrew one hundred dollars, and headed to Paul's house. When I pressed the money into his hand, he couldn't hold back the tears. He said, "My wife and I totally ran out of food last night. We have been up since four o'clock this morning praying for a miracle."

I never missed the one hundred dollars. One thing after another fell into place that allowed me to sustain my family. But no miracle was as great as the one that occurred inside me when I discovered that God truly loves his children and often uses other people to prove it.

❦

Let us fall now into the hand of the Lord;
for his mercies are great.

2 SAMUEL 24:14

Praying for an Accident

*D*uring his senior year in high school, my son Alex began dating a girl named Beth (names changed). Over time, I noticed Alex becoming irritable and curt with family members. Soon, his obstinacy turned to anger. Our relationship, once open and warm, was now terribly strained. My slightest suggestion offended him, and I felt as if I were walking on eggshells whenever we were together.

I suspected that Alex's change of personality had to do with Beth, but I had no idea what was going on. Beth was a beautiful but insecure young woman, a member of the Church, who seemed to be frantically searching for acceptance and love. I sensed that she was determined to marry Alex, no matter what she had to do.

As his mother, I continued to feel anxiety over Alex's well being, but due to our strained relationship, I was unable to discuss my concerns with him. I worried that he was in danger when he was with Beth and that he was vulnerable to her questionable tactics. I felt so helpless. Finally, I turned to God for help. I began praying. I went to my knees many times during the day. I prayed long into the nights. When worry awakened me, I got up and prayed more. I prayed continually for my son's welfare, seeking a solution to this critical situation.

One night, after I had once again taken my concerns to God, I had a dream. I saw Alex facing a twenty-gun firing squad, and amazingly, Beth was the one holding every one of the guns! I awoke from the dream sweating, slid out of bed to my knees, and began to beg God for direction. Presently, a series of impressions flowed into my mind. I became aware that I had only presumed Alex was well informed about proper moral conduct. After all, he had been reared in an active LDS home and had attended church all of his life. Surely he knew the rights and wrongs of dating relationships. But the spiritual feelings told me that my assumptions were incorrect. Alex had indeed heard those principles taught, but he had never internalized them, and that deficiency had now put him at terrible risk. I needed to teach him again in a manner that would plant those principles deeply within his heart, but how? He was spending very little time at home, and when he was home, he was not responsive to my counsel.

I again turned to God for help. I knew that something extraordinary would have to happen to get Alex's attention. I pleaded, "Heavenly Father, Alex is your son, too! Please help me! Please orchestrate circumstances so that Alex's heart will soften and he will become teachable and open to counsel."

The thought came to me, *What you are asking may require your son to experience a difficult situation. Is this what you really want?*

For a few sobering moments, I had to ponder my response. I did not want my child to be hurt, but I knew that something needed to happen quickly to turn him around. I was far more concerned about Alex's eternal welfare than any other consideration. Therefore I answered, "Yes. Even though it may require my son, me, and those I love to endure pain, please do whatever is necessary to soften my son's heart and save his eternal soul."

The following week, an extraordinary event occurred. With little thought of caution, Alex jumped into our family car and pulled onto the highway directly in the path of an approaching van. Our car was struck hard on the passenger side, smashing in the door. The car was instantly totaled. Incredibly, no one was injured, but Alex was terribly shaken and distraught. He knew the accident was his fault. He had to endure the humiliation: the gawking onlookers; the police investigation; the ticket; the apology to the people in the van—and worst of all, he had to explain to us that he had just wrecked our best family automobile.

I learned about the accident from a neighbor. The first thought that entered my mind was, *Alex is all right.* Amazingly, I was not distressed. I was struck with the realization that God's hand was in the event. In fact, I *knew* it was an answer to my prayers!

When I arrived at the scene of the accident, Alex appeared pale. He was trembling. I ran to him and held him in my arms and expressed my love for him. He apologized over and over for his carelessness. I reassured him that we would work things out and that everything would be all right—and I meant it! From that moment, the old Alex began to return. He became sweet, helpful, and patient with family members. He was humble and willing to communicate.

The night following the accident, Alex was working late. I had fallen asleep, but was awakened by the thought, *It is now time for you to teach your son.* Knowing that Alex would soon be arriving home, I went into the living room, knelt by the couch, and prayed for guidance. I realized that it was as important for me to be spiritually prepared to *teach* as it was for Alex to be spiritually prepared to be *taught*.

When Alex walked through the door, he found me on my knees. Assuming that I was worried about him, he softly said, "Mother, I'm sorry I am late. I was just talking with Beth."

"That's all right," I said. "Can we talk for a minute?"

We didn't talk for a minute—we talked until morning. I began by relating to him my concern. I told him about the prayers I had offered in his behalf, the spiritual impressions that had come to me, and the direction that I had received. I explained that I needed to teach him some important principles. He was open and receptive and listened attentively as I explained to him some delicate issues about proprieties in relationships between men and women. I gently expressed my concerns about his relationship with Beth. He asked questions and listened to my answers. During our entire discussion, he never offered a trace of belligerence or resistance.

Within a few days, Alex broke up with Beth. When the weight of their relationship was lifted from his shoulders, Alex was his old self again. He seemed more relaxed and congenial. The experience proved pivotal in his life. He went on to serve an honorable mission, he married in the temple, and he is now the father of a beautiful family.

❧

(For the Lord thy God is a merciful God;) he will not forsake thee,
neither destroy thee, nor forget the covenant of thy fathers.

DEUTERONOMY 4:31

Lost, but Not Forgotten

I was not born an atheist. No one is ever born an atheist. Atheism must be either taught or individually arrived at as a result of life's experiences. For me, the seeds of atheism took root in my early childhood, nurtured by feelings of helplessness and despair that are generated by a life of poverty and homelessness.

My parents were drifters, hitchhikers, living in filthy skid row dives, broken-down trailers, or at times under cardboard. Dad was an alcoholic. In between binges, he would try to get a job as a fry cook or meat cutter. Mom sometimes worked as a waitress, but what little money they earned Dad quickly drank up, or the money was used to pay off bad checks or to bail Dad out of jail. In those days, we used our thumbs for transportation, camped in the desert, and ate bread and cheese when we could obtain them. Except for the sporadic help that we received from the Salvation Army, the Catholic Church, or a kind stranger, we were on our own. Early on, I came to the conclusion that our miserable, nomadic existence was just the way life was; complaining didn't change anything, pleading didn't help, no one was going to rescue us, no one cared—not even God.

When things went from bad to worse, I tried praying to St. Jude, "the patron saint of lost causes," but I gave up and added praying to my list of things that don't work. For me, atheism was a philosophical position that I adopted in a desperate attempt to make sense of the chaos. Atheism was a way that I could put to rest the unanswerable questions of my life, such as, "Why am I here?" and, "Why does life have to be so incredibly difficult?"

At age twenty I found myself exhausted by the futility of life's struggle and convinced that life was absolutely meaningless. Pessimism, despair, a chronic feeling of helplessness, and a disheartening sense of abandonment permeated me each day. I would sometimes stand at an open a window and yell, "Does anybody out there care?" only to become even more depressed as I quietly listened to the silence that followed.

One day, in a small Texas library, I made an incredible discovery. I cried out loud, "All religions were invented by man! The Egyptian sun god, Hinduism, the Greek and Roman gods, Christianity—the whole lot! All of them were created from the imaginations of men!" My sudden outcry disrupted the quiet sanctity of the library, but I didn't care. I felt ecstatic at the discovery, and that was the moment I became an atheist.

Then I felt angry. I felt betrayed by all those who had sent me to God for help. "How could I have let myself be so easily duped?" I asked myself. "I'll never believe in a religion or God again."

I was to keep that vow for almost seventeen years. I didn't become just another run-of-the-mill atheist. I became a *devout* atheist. I became an anti-Christian. As tangible proof of my commitment to atheism, I hung a large three-by-four-foot wooden sign on the wall behind my desk that read, *Thank God I'm an Atheist.* Like Saul of old, I took pleasure in persecuting Christians at every opportunity. I was then teaching at a California college and seldom passed up a chance to humiliate my Christian colleagues and students. If one of my students referred to Jesus in a term paper, I would give him an automatic "C" and toss his paper in the trash. But the Lord never gave up on me, no matter how lost I was and no matter how far I was straying. I began to experience quiet promptings of the Holy Ghost, although I had no idea what was going on.

In the fall of 1977, I began waking up in the middle of the night with the nagging feeling that I was supposed to be doing something. I would get out of bed, flip through my appointment book, and search through my pockets for scraps of paper that might contain a forgotten note. *There is something I am supposed to be doing.* The impression came again and again. I became obsessed with the thought, and I began a frantic search for the answer. The feeling felt urgent. But what was I was supposed to be doing?

I talked incessantly with my wife about the troubling feeling, but could discover no answers, and the intensity of the impression increased. I continued to wake up in the middle of the night, filled with unrelenting anxiety.

The feeling began to interfere with my personal life. My wife and I couldn't go out for a quiet dinner without the feeling intruding.

"Were we supposed to meet someone tonight?" I hesitantly asked her one night.

"No," she answered with a look of concern. "We were not

supposed to meet anyone tonight." Her voice was filled with exasperation. She added, "Nor were we supposed to go *somewhere* else or do *something* different." She took my hand in hers. "I'm not sure I know who you are anymore. Are you okay?"

I tried to reassure her, but I wasn't okay. After we left the restaurant, we drove around for a while; but the uneasy feeling continued. Then something occurred to me. I cautiously asked my wife, "Do you think this feeling has something to do with my father?"

"It's certainly been a long time since you last saw him."

Old, painful memories floated to the surface. The last time I had seen my father was over four years before. I never wanted to see him again. I had no idea where he was. Maybe in Nevada. I shook my head in disbelief. "I can't believe I'm actually trying to find my father."

In retrospect, I realize that I was being prompted to seek out my Heavenly Father, not my earthly father. However, lacking such insight, I began to search for Dad. I started with a call to the police department in Elko. Then I called other county jails in Nevada. Nothing. Dad had disappeared once again, and finding him wasn't going to be easy.

Throughout my childhood, Dad had made a habit of disappearing. As poor as we were, our condition always worsened when Dad abandoned us. Although oppressive poverty and his alcoholism were difficult to endure, Dad's abandoning us was worse, and the most painful part of being abandoned was hearing Mom cry herself to sleep each night. Her torment was beyond her missing him. She knew where he had gone. She told my sister and me that Dad had another wife and family in Fresno, California. I had an older brother, ten years my senior, who had my very same name!

Having had no success finding Dad in Nevada, I nervously decided to contact my half-brother in Fresno to see if he knew where Dad was. He and I had never met. I was now living near Santa Cruz, not far from Fresno. I tentatively dialed his number. Someone answered.

"Hello?" The voice was cheerful, deep, and resonant.

"This is your brother," I said.

"Huh?"

"Your half-brother," I quickly added.

"Well, I'll be . . . really?"

"It's me all right. Surprised?"

Surprised didn't even come close to describing his reaction.

"This is great!" he said. "When can we get together? It's about time we got to know one another."

"I'm in Santa Cruz. Maybe my wife and I could come this weekend."

We talked for a few more minutes, then he said, "I haven't asked you why you called . . ." He paused for a few seconds before continuing. "Has something happened to our dad?"

Our dad was indeed the reason I had called, and I told him that I had hoped that he knew where Dad was.

"Sorry," he said. "The last I heard, Dad was in and out of a hospital in Independence, Missouri. Minor stroke, I think. That was several weeks ago, but I don't know where he is now."

"Thanks," I said. "I'll call some hospitals in Missouri and let you know."

"You can fill me in when you get here this weekend," my brother said.

I finally located the hospital where Dad had been admitted. Only two days before, he had suffered another stroke and had died. Because Dad was a vagrant, the hospital was arranging to bury him in a pauper's grave, but I contacted my half-brother, and he sent money to pay for a proper burial.

When my wife, children, and I arrived at my brother's house, I was not prepared for the big bear hug that he gave me. I fought back tears. Beyond my wife and children, I had never known this kind of love. After the introductions, my wife and I followed my brother to a building on his farm. "Just give me a few more minutes to finish," he said. "I was working on our food storage when you arrived. I have a couple more bags of wheat to seal in these metal drums."

"Why are you storing so much food?" I asked.

"The prophets have recommended that we maintain a year's supply of food, so that's what I'm doing."

Prophets! I turned to my wife and rolled my eyes.

My brother continued to explain. "I'm a Mormon and the prophet of our church has counseled us to store food against times of need."

"Mormon?"

My brother smiled and put his arm around my shoulder. "What religion do you belong to?"

"We don't," I answered bluntly. "I'm an atheist. I chucked the whole religion thing about fifteen years ago. How did you become a Mormon?"

"An interesting story," he replied. "A few months ago I began having a series of strange reoccurring feelings that woke me up in the middle of the night."

"Feelings?" I said, suddenly interested. "What kind of feelings?"

"It was as though I imagined myself walking toward a bright light. I felt drawn to the light, but although I would quicken my pace I never seemed to get any closer to the light. I became aware that I was carrying two books in my hands. I could see that one of them was the Bible, but I couldn't make out the second book. The feelings were driving me crazy. Then a friend of mine—a Mormon—gave me some insight. He immediately knew the identity of the second book. It was the Book of Mormon. My friend asked me if it he could introduce me to a couple of young missionaries. From the outset I knew that what they were telling me was true. Soon, I was baptized, and those feelings have never come back."

"The other book could have been a Sears catalog!" I countered.

"That would be a possibility," he answered, "except for the *other* feeling."

"The *other* feeling?"

"Yes. It's hard to describe. This feeling confirmed the truthfulness of what the missionaries were telling me. I don't know if you've ever had such a feeling, but if you do you'll have no doubt about what it means."

I had to admit that I was fascinated by his story. When our visit ended, my wife and I piled the children in the car and headed for home. Along the way, my wife and I began discussing our visit. We enjoyed our newly found family. My thoughts drifted back to my childhood, hitchhiking, feeling abandoned, and my recent search for my father. I thought about never seeing him again. I thought about my recent sleepless nights and the impression: *There's something you're supposed to be doing.* Then suddenly, a new thought burst upon my consciousness. The impression grew stronger until it consumed me.

I suddenly cried out, "I'm supposed to join that church!" My outburst startled my wife and scared my children. I was so excited that I shouted, "*That's* what I'm supposed to be doing!"

"What are you talking about?" my wife asked.

I pulled to the side of the road. "I'm supposed to join the Mormon Church!" I said. "Don't you see? I have that *feeling.*"

"What feeling?"

"My brother said when I had that special feeling I would know what it meant. I know what it means!"

"But you're a confirmed atheist!" my wife said.

No matter. My mind was set. I had never been so sure or excited about anything in my life. When we arrived home in Santa Cruz I was ready to join. I looked for "Mormon Church" in the phone book but couldn't find it. My wife told me that the real name was The Church of Jesus Christ of Latter-day Saints, which I thought was quite a mouthful. I arranged for the missionaries to come and teach our family the lessons. I asked them questions that had plagued me throughout my life: Why are we here? Why is there so much suffering in the world? If there is a God, does he care about what happens to us? I asked about the eternal nature of the family, a subject that was of prime importance to me now. The *what-am-I-supposed-to-be-doing?* feeling had now completely vanished, and I was sleeping like a baby.

We began to attend a ward on Sundays. The missionaries patiently taught us the principles of the gospel, one by one. A few weeks later, we were baptized. At the baptismal service, it was announced that my brother *of the same name* would baptize me, and it was announced that we were the sons of a father *of the same name.* An explanatory note was entered on the bottom of my baptismal record so that no one would suspect that I had baptized myself.

I am continually amazed to realize that God knew me, had watched over me, and had loved me throughout those difficult years of drifting, homelessness, abandonment, and abuse. He reached out to me even when I fought against him, and he rescued me from a distance that I thought could not be spanned.

❧

How think ye? if a man have an hundred sheep, and one of them be gone astray, doth he not leave the ninety and nine, and goeth into the mountains, and seeketh that which is gone astray? And if so be that he find it, verily I say unto you, he rejoiceth more of that sheep, than of the ninety and nine which went not astray. Even so it is not the will of your Father which is in heaven, that one of these little ones should perish.

MATTHEW 18:12–14

Turning Away from the Bunkhouse and the Cowboy

I had been trying to change for years. . . . well . . . I had been *praying* to change for years, but I never could quite succeed in giving up behaviors that I knew were wrong. To put it delicately, I had an addiction to wanting attention from men, and I had struggled for a very long time with getting myself into compromising situations. I really wanted to do better, but I could never stop myself from turning down destructive offers that gave me the attention I craved. I always felt terrible afterwards. Before my dates I would pray, "Please don't let me do anything bad. Please help me to say no." Then I would allow myself to go out with some lowlife who was only interested in satisfying his selfish desires.

The summer after my first year of college, I went to work at a dude ranch. I really wanted to put my past behind me once and for all. I had recently met a good man whom I thought I might marry, and I wanted to overcome my problems and feel worthy of him. But . . . dude ranch . . . cowboys . . . big problems just waiting to happen. One of the cowboys began inviting me up to his bunkhouse on a regular basis, and I started going. Each time I resolved that I would never do anything bad. But deep inside I knew I was lying to myself.

Late one night, when I was heading to his bunkhouse, I prayed, "Please bless me that nothing will happen." Then I *felt* a voice speaking to me, saying, "I can't help you until you turn yourself around. Then I will run to meet you."

I stopped dead in my tracks. A war began to rage within me. The attention addict part of me desperately wanted to go the bunkhouse, but the repentant part of me wanted more to be embraced by God. After a long struggle, I knew what I had to do; I knew it was "my moment." I turned around. It was so hard. I took one step, then another, and finally, one step at a time, I arrived back at my room. I felt an incredible peace and acceptance, as though God was indeed there to welcome me and that he had helped me to get home.

After that night, I was a changed person. I never again went to the bunkhouse or anywhere else that I shouldn't. I always felt God near me, encouraging me, and helping me keep my resolve. Later, I married that "good" man, who has loved me unconditionally. He took me to the temple, and we have lived happily with God as the central part of our lives.

❧

And I answered him, saying: Yea, it is the love of God, which sheddeth itself abroad in the hearts of the children of men; wherefore, it is the most desirable above all things.

1 Nephi 11:22

Miracle at Sea

The final diagnosis was an acute ulcer. Any internal bleeding for a hemophiliac, especially in 1955, was considered serious, even life-threatening.

My husband, Ralph, and I were two days out of LeHavre, France, on the SS *Samaria,* returning to the United States following a European tour with the Tabernacle Choir. We had been talking with some friends on the deck of the ship when Ralph began to complain that he was feeling ill and retired to our cabin. A few hours later, he became very sick to his stomach. He sat up in bed and vomited two quarts of blood in a basin. I immediately ran up two flights of stairs to the doctor's quarters for help. When the doctor hurried back with me and saw the blood in the basin, he exclaimed, "Oh, no! OH, NO!"

Ralph needed an infusion of whole blood now, but there was no supply on board the ship and there was no cross-matching equipment to test donors. Giving him the wrong type of blood, of course, would likely kill him. The doctor did the next best thing by giving Ralph a transfusion of three pints of pooled plasma. But the hemorrhaging continued. Finally, the doctor had no choice except to risk calling for donors and giving transfusions of whole blood. We knew that Ralph had O Positive blood, and we began a frantic search throughout the ship for anyone who believed he or she had that blood type. When we had gathered a group of probable donors, the doctor began giving Ralph what was to be a long series of trans-fusions—fifteen in all.

I cannot express the anxiety I felt as each new batch was admin-istered to my husband, each one suspect and potentially lethal. All I could do was offer a silent prayer over each donation and hope that the donor was not mistaken about his blood type.

As news of Ralph's struggle for life spread throughout the ship, a collective effort was made by passengers of diverse backgrounds to petition God for help. The members of the Tabernacle Choir fasted, and some passengers fasted with us. One woman said to me, "I am not a praying person, but I want to pray for your husband now." Another man said, "I am old, but I asked God to take some of my strength and give it to Ralph so he could live." Such support buoyed me. But just as the miracle of the transfusions was beginning to save his life, another adversity was to threaten it.

A violent storm broke upon the ship. The sea became terribly rough, and the crew informed us that the conditions would persist for another 48 hours. Our ship was tossed to and fro, almost helpless against the turbulence. Many people became seasick. The fierce pitching of the ship caused Ralph to lose more blood, and soon he became so ill that one of his lungs collapsed. Fearing for his life, I begged the doctor to summon a seaplane to fly him to a hospital.

"The waves are thirty feet high," the doctor said. "A plane would be dashed to pieces."

Now, one truth became obvious to us all: Without the ocean calming, Ralph would die. I asked the members of the Choir and many of the people that had supported us to come together and pray for the storm to cease. I had never offered such an urgent prayer. We waited and watched. Within the hour, the storm abated. A friend came to Ralph's room in the infirmary and motioned me to look out the porthole at the glassy, calm water. The sun had just broken through the clouds, beautiful, bright, and clear. My friend said, "Did you ever see such a beautiful sea?"

The calm provided Ralph a respite for the night, and his condition stabilized for a few hours. Then, early in the morning, his body began to fail. His heart started beating so rapidly that the doctor couldn't make an accurate count. Suddenly, Ralph's heart stopped altogether. As the doctor feverishly worked to revive him, I stood back and pled with the Lord to intervene. Again, my prayers were urgent. I knew that only God could help.

Within a few moments, the doctor managed to revive Ralph, but for the next 36 hours Ralph was to face the worst period of his battle for life. Barely conscious now, he held my hand limply and said he didn't know if he had the strength to hang on. He said he felt as though his spirit was fighting to leave his body, that if he let up for just one moment his spirit would slip away.

During that 36-hour period, Ralph's heart stopped three more times and he had to be given adrenalin to bring him back. After each episode, the doctor tried to prepare me by saying, "Your husband doesn't have a chance of living through this. I cannot give you any hope." But my prayers and the prayers of many others continued. Throughout the entire ordeal, good people throughout the ship continued to petition God and to fast. They lined up to offer more of their blood. Each time, I prayed that they had made no mistake about their blood type. As the passengers joined in our fight for Ralph's life, I fought to drive out all doubt and to place my trust in my Heavenly Father, with whom nothing is impossible. I kept saying to myself, "I will not believe what the doctor says."

On Thursday morning Ralph "died" and was resuscitated yet one more time. When he regained consciousness, he turned toward me, so weak that he could hardly speak. He was perspiring profusely. I sat beside him, weeping, stroking his forehead.

"What chances have I got?" he asked me. His tone was that of weariness. He seemed to have no fight left in him. Before I could answer, Ralph closed his eyes and fell into a deep, peaceful sleep. I bowed my head there at his bedside and a feeling came to me as if to say, *He has suffered enough.*

When Ralph awoke four hours later, he had renewed energy to fight for his life, and from that moment on he began to improve. On Friday morning, a nurse came into the infirmary, opened the curtains, and let the sun stream into the room. Ralph wept like a child. He said, "I thought I would never see the sun again."

Then the nurse began to cry. She said to me, "I've never seen anything so amazing in my life. At four o'clock this morning I was sure he wouldn't make it, and now look at him! I will never again doubt that miracles are possible."

I shall always remember that Saturday morning when Ralph was wheeled from the *SS Samaria* to a waiting ambulance in Quebec. The entire side of the ship was crowded with 1,200 friends—Choir members, crew, passengers, and medical staff—who had fought for Ralph and prayed for him. They waved, applauded, and cheered us. That memory and the knowledge of the infinite goodness of God will last us a lifetime.

❧

Yet will I not forget thee. Behold, I have graven
thee upon the palms of my hands.

ISAIAH 49:15–16

The Miracle of a Mother's Love

When parents adopt, they often receive special spiritual indications that let them know that they and the child were guided to each other. Prayers reach God's ears and matches are made. Such was our case.

Years ago, it was the law in our state that adoptive parents were not allowed to visit the newborn baby in the hospital. The little boy that my husband and I were to adopt was born three weeks early and weighed only 4½ pounds. He was losing weight daily because he wouldn't drink from a bottle. We spent five agonizing days being told by the adoption lawyer that the child was not doing well and that he wouldn't eat.

I finally said, "I'm his mother and he needs me. Get me into that hospital." The attorney again refused to grant permission, and I told him, "Get me in legally or I will have to break the law. My baby needs me now!"

He found a way.

My husband and I were allowed into the hospital within a very short time. As we moved toward the isolation unit where the child was being tended, we both offered urgent prayers that our baby would respond to us. A doctor and two nurses met us and told us to scrub and dress in sterile hospital gowns. When we entered the room, we saw our tiny son for the first time. My heart swelled with love for him. I said to a nurse, "Please let me feed him." She gently placed the baby in my arms and handed me his bottle.

"He won't eat," she said, her voice filled with worry.

With tears in my eyes I looked into his beautiful little face and tenderly said, "I'm your mother, and I love you. Please eat for me." Then I put the bottle to his mouth and he immediately began sucking. The doctor and nurses were astonished. Tears flowed down everyone's cheeks. Then my husband held the child and it ate for him.

For two days, I went to the hospital for each feeding, and soon he was released into our care. What a miracle from God to let us know by this means that he had chosen us to be the child's parents and that this baby was indeed ours.

❧

I know that he loveth his children.

1 NEPHI 11:17

Praying for Your Enemies

My cousin had been like my sister. We couldn't have been closer. We had raised our families together, picnicked, played games, laughed, and loved each other. It had been a long and wonderful relationship blessed by heaven. I had been closer to her than I had been to my own siblings. She had been my dearest friend. I loved to hear her rattle off books that she had read and proffer philosophy. We shared a love for movies and challenged each other's trivia prowess. More than once, when I had not been able to make ends meet, she had shown up with a wad of cash and a hug. I was the first one she called when her mother died. Later, when my mother was dying, I sought her out for comfort and counsel.

Then we tried to start a business together. We couldn't have made a worse mistake. Our goals and philosophies were divergently opposite. Friction rather than love filled our days. We began steering clear of each other and speaking only when we needed to. We found ourselves biting our tongues to avoid saying out loud the hurtful things we were thinking. Dark feelings began to permeate our work environment, and we took the bad sentiments home at night. We were stuck. We had made the terrible error of marrying our finances and our futures together, and now we were miserable.

One day I exploded with anger. I said hateful things that cut deeply. She retaliated with scathing criticism. We stood nose to nose, glared at each other, and screamed demonic, ugly things that could not be taken back. She ordered me away from the office, and I never returned. Just like that, our business and our relationship were over. Now, my dearest friend in the world had become my worst enemy. Our love had turned to hatred. Thereafter, the mere thought of her caused me to shake with anger. I seethed and ruminated, regurgitating then chewing the foul-tasting cud of hate. Each time I relived the horrible event, I found myself imagining worse things that I could have said or done. *Why couldn't I have thought of such and such to say? That would have shown her!* But my mind hadn't been quick enough at the time. Now all I could do was imagine and boil.

Months passed. Hatred must be fed; it has no life of its own. Maintaining hate is exhausting. Tending bad feelings requires enormous effort. I couldn't keep it up. I found myself longing for peace. I wanted relief. Soon, I began to have feelings of shame. I had learned something ugly about myself, and I wasn't proud of it. In a moment of careless selfishness, I had thrown out the window everything that I had cherished about the virtues of charity and forgiveness. I had smugly believed that I was immune from such un-Christ-like behavior. A tug-of-war was raging within me. On the one hand my injured ego still wanted to be soothed; on the other hand that was not what was suffering. I could not hide from the guilt of knowing that my part of the confrontation had been wrong. But I couldn't think of a way to repair the damage.

I turned to prayer. Surely the Atonement could provide a solution. But how? I made the matter the subject of scripture study, fasting, and temple attendance.

Then one day I had a breakthrough.

I was reading the words of Zenos in Alma 33:4: "Thou wast merciful when I prayed concerning those who were mine enemies, and thou didst turn them to me."

Instantly, I was filled with hope. I realized that an "enemy" is not necessarily a person who is trying to destroy me; an enemy could be someone with whom I have a grievance. Considering that definition, my cousin was my enemy! I began to cross-reference and found that the scriptures were filled with information about praying for your enemies. The answer was always the same: If you are willing to change your heart, the Lord will either soften the heart of your enemy or turn your enemy out of your path. One way or another, you will be delivered.

I began praying for my cousin, my enemy. I reevaluated my life and made new commitments about charitable gospel living. I prayed that her heart would be softened toward me and that the Lord would present me with a way to make peace or at least come to peace.

It was the Christmas season now. I was driving down a busy street and suddenly I saw my cousin driving toward me in the opposite lane. I had neither seen nor talked to her in a year. My heart began beating hard and fast. My first feeling was anger; I wanted to look away. But as I forced myself to clap eyes on hers, I felt a gentle urging that gave me the courage to do what is right. I waved and smiled. To my astonishment, she returned the gestures. And then she was gone. But in that brief split second, we had made contact—friendly contact.

Did I have the courage to take the next step? I wondered.

During the next several weeks, as I shopped the stores for family Christmas presents, I considered sending my cousin an "olive branch." After all, this was the season of peace and goodwill. Maybe the spirit of Christmas could repair a relationship that had been so badly damaged. With that in mind, I soon found the perfect gift. It was small and inexpensive, but it clearly fit my cousin's personality. As I wrapped it, I signed a simple card. "I hope this simple gift will bring cheer to your Christmas season. With love . . ."

That was all it said.

I summoned courage. I did not know how the present would be received. Sending it meant I would have to let go of the hostility within me; it meant the death of my longtime companion, *hate*. After I mailed the gift, I would no longer be able to hold onto my pride. The present carried with it a message that I was admitting to some of the blame for our differences, something I had not been willing to do.

Mailing the present was a risk.

Maybe she would toss it out with the trash.

Maybe she would expect me to admit fault for the entire affair.

Maybe this is just what she had been waiting for—*vindication!*

Maybe my gift would just add fuel to an already very hot fire.

As I dropped the package in the mailbox, I decided I couldn't be responsible for her reaction. *Do what is right; let the consequence follow.* I had prayed for my enemy; I had repented of my shortcomings; and now I had sent all my hopes in a small package. I had done all that I could.

Christmas came and went. The joys of family and the bustle of the season temporarily drowned out my thoughts of my cousin's response. Then, just before New Year's, I answered a knock at the door. A young man was standing there with a big bouquet of flowers in his hands. Stunned, I took it, opened the accompanying envelope, and read the card.

"You always know just what I love," it read.

The season of hatred was over. We were once more sisters. Love had not been lost; it had only been postponed. God had repaired our relationship when there had been no hope of reconciliation. All was restored. We have gone on with life and we never speak of the incident. It is as distant as though it had never happened. No scars. No hurt. Only God could do that.

❧

The Lord is merciful and gracious, slow to anger,
and plenteous in mercy.
PSALM 103:8

Rescued Onboard Ship

Twenty-eight years ago, a U.S. Navy cruiser was entering the Indian Ocean for a sixty-day at-sea patrol. Onboard was a 35-year-old, inactive Latter-day Saint sailor, a user of alcohol and tobacco and a willing participant in other vices that were spiritually diminishing. I was that sailor.

At 2200 hours, I made my way out onto the dark deck. After my eyes adjusted to the blackness, and after making certain I was alone, I sank to my knees and prayed for almost half an hour that the Lord would help me to straighten out my life and enable me to overcome my bad habits. I was a defeated man, almost 12,000 miles away from home. I knew I had not lived the principles that I had been taught in my youth. My rebellion had brought me only misery.

In my teens, I had made bad decisions—lots of them. Now I had no one to blame but myself. My parents had set outstanding examples for me. My dad was a good, spiritual, dedicated man and a super father. Mother taught me the gospel by word and deed. She loved me unconditionally. When I started down the wrong road, my parents suffered intense emotional and even physical pain. All they could do was stand by and watch me grow more and more inactive in the gospel and trample every teaching that they had tried to instill in me. I had known the things that I was doing were wrong. Who could not? I remember seeing the hurt in their eyes as they begged me to stop using tobacco and alcohol. They felt so helpless.

But they never gave up on me; they never stopped praying for me. I always knew I was loved. After I enlisted in the Navy at age 22, I received a letter from my mother each and every week for the 7½ years that I was away. She expressed her affection for me; she spoke freely of her love for the gospel; and she gently encouraged me to give up my bad habits and to come back to Church.

That night, as I concluded my prayer and arose from my knees, I resolved then and there to stop using tobacco and alcohol. This time I would choose to do right!

The next morning my craving for a cigarette was so overwhelming that I was ready to give up on my resolution. I headed below deck to the ship's store to buy another pack. *I have been kidding myself,* I thought; *I will never be able to quit.* Just then, the ship's loudspeaker screeched, ordering all hands' attention. The boatswain mate announced, "Now hear this: LDS services are now being held in the ship's library."

I paused and looked around. I was standing only ten feet from the library door! Suddenly, a thought rushed into my mind, *You asked for help . . . this is it.*

I stepped to the door and slowly opened it. A smiling LDS group leader met me. He offered me his hand. I heard a long-forgotten hymn being played on a small organ. The group leader led me into the room where eight other LDS men welcomed me. The meeting was simple but familiar. The sacrament was blessed and passed; a lesson was taught; a benediction was offered. As I stood to leave, the group leader came to me and said, "Brother, I have the distinct impression that we need to talk. Would you stay and visit with me for a few minutes?" He was eleven years my junior and a returned missionary. His calling was to be the leader for all the LDS men onboard. I stayed. We visited. He went the extra mile and helped me come home.

From that moment to this I have remained active in the Church and have tried to serve to the best of my ability. I especially keep my eye out for the one who seems lost and far from home. I know from my own experience that patient love and the timely hand of fellowship will rescue even a soul as rebellious and proud as mine. The love of God is constantly available to even the most lost among us. Miracles really do happen!

❧

We love him, because he first loved us.

1 John 4:19

Two Navajo Women of Faith

The Navajo people have a simple but effective belief in God. They seem to know instinctively that he loves them and will bless them. Years ago, while serving a mission among the Navajos, I was both a witness to and a participant in two extraordinary events.

Many of the pastoral Navajos have a custom: The daughters sometimes *donate* a child to the grandparents to rear. As this child grows, it is trained to be a shepherd and to herd the sheep of the aging grandparents.

Six months into my mission to the Navajo people in Arizona, I was assigned to a new part of the mission where many Church members were scattered over a wide expanse of desert. Some were far removed from the nearest branch and had no transportation. Regular church attendance was almost impossible. One of our jobs as missionaries was to visit these remote members and take the blessings of the gospel to them.

Near the edge of a canyon, about 85 miles from Tomb City, an old grandmother lived with her 3-year-old granddaughter. Their dwelling was a coarse, earth-covered hogan, which holding to tradition was built with the entrance facing east. My companion and I periodically visited this sister and her granddaughter. When we called on her in the fall, we looked around, but didn't see the child playing.

"Where's the girl?" we asked.

"In the hogan—sick," she replied.

We stepped inside the small quarters and saw a little, brown-skinned girl lying on a blanket with thick, yellow scabs and an eruption of oozing sores on over 80 percent of her body—impetigo! We knew that this contagious bacterial skin infection could kill the child.

"Give her a blessing," the grandmother said. I looked at the child and felt a shock of fear. My 20-year-old mind suddenly reviewed every reason why this wouldn't work. But the old grandmother was determined. *Give her a blessing.* She had no doubt. We held the priesthood of God, and God would heal the child—it was as simple as that.

My companion and I gave the child a priesthood blessing. What else could we do?

But throughout the day and for several days following I was nervous. I was so concerned that the child might die that I arranged with my companion to visit them again. We returned four days later. When we arrived, to my astonishment and relief, I saw the little girl in front of the Hogan playing in the sand. Her skin was mostly clear of the infection!

As I contemplated the weight of the miracle I had witnessed, one thing became painfully obvious to me: This old woman, who could seldom attend Church meetings, knew more about faith in Jesus

Christ than did I. Her example taught me a great lesson in believing in the priesthood of God that had been entrusted to me.

I would see that kind of faith again.

My companion and I were visiting a member in the hospital in Tomb City. Suddenly, we heard a great commotion and saw an 84-year-old Navajo woman running down the hall toward us. We knew her. Like many of the Church members, she herded sheep in a remote area. She had no child to help her. She wove rugs for additional income while caring for her invalid husband who was nearly blind. Recently, she had become very ill—coughing up mucus, running a fever, losing weight, and suffering chest pains—and neighbors had brought her to the hospital. The old man had been left at their hogan.

When she ran toward us, she had effectively fought off all attempts of the medical personnel to restrain her. She wanted to get to the elders. She didn't understand what was happening to her, she said. She had been admitted into the hospital, and now, after tests had been taken, she was being sent to another facility at Fort Defiance where she was to be isolated.

Her inability to speak English and the doctors' limited knowledge of Navajo had complicated the situation. She was wide-eyed with agitation. Her wrinkled, weatherworn face looked older and grayer than usual, if that was possible. We tried to comfort her and stepped aside to consult with the doctors.

Tuberculosis!

We were shown the X rays. We were asked to explain to her the serious nature of her condition. In order to save her life, the doctors needed to remove and isolate her—now!

Who is prepared to tell someone that her condition is potentially terminal? As gently as we could, my companion and I tried to relay the doctors' explanations to a trembling old woman who was struggling to comprehend. We held up her X rays and pointed out the dark shadows on the lungs. The disease is infectious, we said; the sickness is now in the lungs and will spread to other parts of the body.

"I need a blessing," she said. "I need to return to my hogan to tend my husband and the sheep. They cannot survive without me."

Debating the issue with her did little good. The more we tried to convince her that she should follow the doctors' instructions the more insistent she became. She appreciated the doctors, she said, but she would trust the elders to ask God if he would heal her.

"Give me a blessing and all will be well," she pled.

We gave her a blessing.

The minute we were finished, she began to tug at her hospital admittance bracelet. The doctors had now hurried to stop her. "What are you doing?" they asked.

"I'm okay now. I can go home to take care of my old man," she said.

Perhaps realizing that they were in a predicament that would require force to keep her, the doctors suggested that they take additional X rays to reconfirm her condition. The old Navajo woman reluctantly agreed. When the doctors returned with the film, her lungs were shown to be completely clear. She was released and went home.

Over the years I have reflected many times on these events and how the faith of two Navajo women shaped my conviction of the love of God for his children. I have listened to inspiring speakers and have sat at the feet of great leaders, but these women in the remote desert of Arizona taught me abiding faith.

I will mention the lovingkindnesses of the Lord, and the praises of the Lord, according to all that the Lord hath bestowed on us . . . according to his mercies, and according to the multitude of his lovingkindnesses.

Isaiah 63:7

A Good Trade

$\mathcal{G}$od's solution is not always ours. I grew up in a family with enough but little extra. When my brother was nearing mission age, my parents had the money neither to send nor to support him. Our family prayers began to focus on this problem. Morning and night, as a young girl, I joined in those heartfelt pleadings. Our constant request was that the Lord would open a way for my brother to be able to serve a mission.

As provider of the family, my father took the matter extra-seriously. He felt that he should be able to come up with a way to send his son on a mission, but he kept coming up short. My father was an electrician, and he had tried everything from taking on extra work to selling household items to solve the dilemma. Still he could find no way to finance the mission. Finally, at the point of despair, he went off by himself and implored the Lord for a solution. As he prayed, he promised that he would do or give anything. No sacrifice would be too much.

The Lord took him at his word.

Shortly thereafter, just before Christmas, he was installing a steel box on a pole. Suddenly, a splinter of steel flew off the metal box and struck him in the eye. He was rushed to the hospital where the doctor was able to extract the splinter, but Dad had to remain in the hospital for a week.

Dad lost the sight in that injured eye. The entire incident was discouraging for the family. I think we all silently wondered about the irony of praying for extra funds for a mission only to have the family's breadwinner incapacitated. Dad was unable to work or earn income for a month. During that time our attention turned from my brother's mission to Dad's health. Our faith was shaken. We had more questions than answers. Just like Dad, we were blind to God's purposes. But six months later our vision began to improve.

Nothing short of a miracle turned the tide of adversity. An insurance claim was suddenly honored, and Dad began receiving compensation for the loss of his eye. Money was sent to him each month for two years. Almost to the penny the compensation checks amounted to the cost of my brother's mission. Remarkably, the insurance payments began when my brother left on his mission and ended when he returned.

I never heard my father complain about the accident. He always said it was a good trade—his eye for my brother's mission. When there had been no other solution, my father had the faith to take his problem to the Lord and offered to make any sacrifice. Though he would be blind in one eye the rest of his life, he was always grateful that the Lord had answered his prayer. My father loved his son and the Lord loved my father—that's all there was to it: two demonstrations of love that I shall never forget.

❧

Yea, I have loved thee with an everlasting love.

JEREMIAH 31:3

Welcome Home

Two months after we were married, my husband was diagnosed with Crohn's Disease. In an emergency operation, eighteen inches of his intestine were removed. From that point forward, Crohns became a third member of our marriage, and the hospital became our second home.

Home. That word became foreign to us. During our first years of marriage, strangling medical debt dictated our residences and moves. Now we had a baby girl. More poor health and meager finances forced us to move once again, this time in with family. The three of us crowded into two tiny bedrooms that our parents graciously provided in their house.

Later, when we thought that the Crohns was in remission, we decided that education was our only hope for normalcy. So we moved—again. This time to be students. Our excitement to finally be on our own was short-lived, however. Too soon, we discovered that the college program we wanted required unethical practices of its students in exchange for grades. To live our values or to leave school were our choices. We packed up and left.

When we returned to our parents' home and the two cramped bedrooms, we felt defeated. Then my husband's Crohns took a frightening and deep dive. Suddenly we had to face the difficult realization that his current health status would not allow him to maintain a full-time job. I would need to become the primary breadwinner, and our prospects for affording a place of our own now seemed worse than ever. And, of course, the medical debts kept mounting.

We wanted to be self-sufficient; we wanted to be an independent family. We did not want to be reliant upon others. So we prayed. We knew that no one could get us through this except Heavenly Father.

Slowly, things began to change. Within a short period of time we received a government grant and an unexpectedly large tax return. Suddenly we could pay off our medical debts! Then I received a job offer; then a few months later a better one; and then a few months later a better one yet. But our living situation had not improved— two cramped bedrooms in our parent's house.

One night I prayed again. I didn't want to be ungrateful. I knew that one thing after another had been working out. I knew where our blessings were coming from. I hoped I wouldn't be asking amiss.

For some time I had longed for and pictured in my mind a sweet little apartment that we could live in—a modest place with some elbowroom, a yard with green grass, a safe neighborhood, a nice ward, and a friend for my little girl . . . and it all had to fit into our meager budget. By scrimping we might be able to come up with $650 a month for my dream place.

Unlikely. Impossible. These words had kept me from offering the prayer before.

But this night I yearned for change, and I knew I could not achieve it on my own. I humbly took my request to Heavenly Father. I imagined that it was too much to ask. But I asked anyway.

The next day, my sister called. Her brother- and sister-in-law were just finishing building a new home, she said. It had a large basement apartment. It had a huge green yard. It was in a nice part of town, and the ward was wonderful. A little girl, the same age as our daughter, lived next door. They were willing to rent the apartment for only $650 a month!

Suddenly what I had thought could never change had changed. What I had imagined impossible had become possible. When I first walked into my "dream apartment," I felt as though *Someone* had already been there. It was as though someone had placed a little note on the door saying, *Welcome home.*

❧

The Lord God [is] merciful and gracious, longsuffering,
and abundant in goodness and truth.
EXODUS 34:6

The Power, Knowledge, and Love of God

I have loved you, saith the Lord.

MALACHI 1:2

A Story That Must Be Told

Compiler's Note: We conclude with a remarkable story that demonstrates the power, foreknowledge, and love of God. Because the incidents so clearly reveal God's guidance and intervention, the details of this lengthy account are left intact. Married couples face few challenges as difficult as infertility. This is the story of two miracle children who came to a faithful couple as pure gifts from God.

As newlyweds, infertility was the last thing we expected to face. Both my wife and I had come from large, "double-digit" families. To us, having a home filled with children was synonymous with marriage. Although we were poor college students at the time, we wanted to begin our family, and we set out fully confident that a large posterity was our future.

Then nothing. No baby.

We tried unsuccessfully for a year and a half to achieve a pregnancy while we watched family members and friends bringing beautiful children into the world. As we experienced one negative pregnancy test after another, our patience wore thin. We fasted, sought inspiration in the temple, and counseled with our parents and church leaders. Having a baby became the primary focus of our prayers. But our pleadings seemed to bounce off the ceiling. We wondered why God would ignore us when all we wanted to do was keep our temple covenants.

In January, a most discouraging time, I asked my father to give both my wife and me a priesthood blessing. A specific promise was given that was to become our anchor: *You will have natural children, and a pregnancy will occur within a year's time.* With hope renewed, we spent the next twelve months pleading with the Lord that the promise be fulfilled.

Time crept like a tortoise. Each month we prepared for a positive pregnancy test, but every time the results came back negative. Nevertheless, we tried to maintain a positive outlook and keep our faith in God.

During that trying year, we received an unexpected letter from the Social Security Administration directing me to reapply for some benefits. I had dealt with health challenges most of my life and had previously received some disability and schooling aid. When my employment status had changed, I had assumed that I would not qualify for the benefits, so I had not corresponded with Social Security for months. The day that I read their letter, I quickly discarded it and threw it onto a stack of junk mail on a corner of my desk. After several weeks, my efficient wife asked me about the letter. It was a waste of time, I said. It wouldn't hurt to try, she replied. I reluctantly jotted down the required information, stuffed it in an envelope, and stuck a stamp on it. Then we took off on a much-needed five-day vacation.

After we returned home and sorted through our mail, we found to our surprise a check from Social Security for $3,000! The check was for back payments that Social Security owed me. Our minds began to race. We were poor students. We imagined all the things we could buy. But we both had the strong impression not to spend the funds. Instead, we deposited the full amount in a savings account.

The end of the year was rapidly approaching, and the promised blessing of a baby had not come. We decided to seek out an infertility specialist to advise us and we soon learned of a doctor who was well known for her success where others had failed, but an appointment was months in the future. We prayed that the Lord would help us get in to see her more quickly. Within a short period of time our prayers were answered. We received a phone call from the doctor's office informing us of a cancellation. We were so astounded and grateful! We had no doubt that the Lord was helping us. Now we felt a tiny glimmer of hope. We were piling up more and more evidence that God cared about us and that he was guiding us step by step over rugged and uncertain terrain. *Finally,* we thought, *a specialist will identify our infertility problem and we can pursue treatment options.*

No one is prepared to hear that he or she is infertile. We had awaited the results of our tests nervously. Then we received an answer in the mail. On the fertility scale, I was practically nonexistent. My wife and I cried. We couldn't help it. This news was beyond a trial of faith. The priesthood blessing had been wrong, or the Lord had let us down, or both. I got in the car and drove. I was depressed. I thought of myself as a failure as a man. I could not give my wife a child—and there was nothing anyone could do about it. I tried to pray, but I couldn't form the words. My mind was a blank. I could find no peace. I felt as though I was being crushed by my burdens. I finally looked heavenward and cried out, "Haven't we been tested enough?" But there was no answer, just silence.

That night, we decided to visit our parents. Armed with *the letter,* we sat down with my wife's mother and showed her the results. Our emotions migrated from frustration to anger to sadness to confusion. We could not understand what the Lord was doing to us. We even wondered out loud if he makes promises *casually* and keeps them *occasionally.* Then my mother-in-law stopped us cold. She said something that we will never forget: *God keeps his promises!*

We quit complaining and listened to her bear her testimony. Here sat a wise woman who had reared a large family and had suffered for years with every imaginable pain throughout her body. She, too, had received assurances through priesthood blessings and, although she was not yet healed, she fully trusted that God would fulfill his promises. She felt the Lord had a plan for us, and she encouraged us not to give up hope.

Somewhat buoyed, my wife and I drove to my parents' home. They were also shocked at the news. I told my father that I couldn't understand why the Lord would promise us through a priesthood blessing that a pregnancy would occur within a year and then, on almost the exact anniversary of that blessing, give us the discouraging news that our chances of ever having children were zero. What had we hoped, fasted, and prayed for during the past year? Why bother asking the Lord for help if he doesn't intend to help you? Why request a priesthood blessing if it probably won't work? What did we have to show for our trusting God? Obviously, our testimonies had been shaken. We were trying hard to reestablish a definable foundation for our faith, but we were in a free fall, and we were desperately looking for a net.

Interestingly, our venting brought us full circle, and late that evening we reached up to God for answers and asked my father for another priesthood blessing. Dad laid his hands on our heads, first one and then the other, and spoke in the name of the Lord. He promised peace, direction, and assurance that the Lord was in charge . . . and that *children would come into our home!* Following the blessing, he asked if we had considered adoption. But we were still too emotional to entertain other options that evening. We needed time to regroup. We left my parents' home exhausted but somewhat reassured, even though we were clueless about how the pieces of this puzzle would ever fit together.

The Adoption Option

As we explored options with our fertility doctor, the news went from bad to worse. That I would never father a child was clearly stated as a fact of life. We would need to learn to deal with it and move on. My low fertility number even ruled out extreme alternatives such as artificial insemination and in vitro fertilization. Even so, the cost would have been prohibitive: $8,000 to $10,000 per attempt. The doctor told my wife and me that either donor insemination or adoption would be our best bet.

Our drive home was filled with discussion. We knew that Church leaders had discouraged the donor insemination option, so we quickly rejected it. But as we discussed adoption, we quickly received a strong, positive impression. We were both surprised at the immediate clarity of thought, although we had no clue about adoption opportunities or procedures. We suddenly felt driven to pursue the adoption process as quickly as possible. We made an appointment with LDS Family Services and met with a wonderful adoption worker who gave us all the information we needed.

During that time, a strange thing happened. My wife was sitting in a stake conference session, pondering the former priesthood blessing promise that a pregnancy would occur within a year. Suddenly, she received an impression that perhaps the pregnancy *had* occurred within that timeframe—but not with her. Maybe she was not to be the birthmother; and maybe our child was already on the way! When she related this thought to me, we both felt the Spirit confirm that this impression was correct. The puzzle pieces were beginning to fit together. Our faith was finding solid ground again, and we were beginning to realize that the Lord was truly in charge and that he had every intention of keeping his promises.

Another amazing thing occurred, another sign of God's foreknowledge and active involvement in our lives. As we were working through the adoption application process, our counselor told us that, in our situation, the cost of adoption would be $3,000. Then we remembered the miracle money from Social Security that we had felt inspired not to spend, but to save—exactly $3,000! We were so grateful to the Lord that he had anticipated our adoption expenses far in advance. With the application process completed and the deposit paid, LDS Family Services approved us, and we were then placed in the pool of adoptive applicants who were waiting to be selected by a birthmother.

An Inspired Visiting Teacher

During a discouraging period, a remarkable visiting teacher came into the life of my wife. Her name was Linda. This sweet young woman had recently miscarried; it was her second miscarriage. She longed for children. As Linda and my wife talked and embraced, my wife shared with Linda the struggles that we had been having and how we had now turned to adoption. They both wept for each other and for the children they hoped to have.

One day, Linda came to my wife and said that she wanted to fast and pray with her. My wife reluctantly agreed. Fasting literally makes her sick, and at the time, she didn't believe that fasting would do very much good. But the next Sunday they fasted together. After church, Linda came to our apartment to break the fast and pray. They talked for a while. Then they knelt together in the living room. My wife offered a prayer and then Linda offered one. Linda prayed that if somewhere there was an unwed, pregnant girl who was weighing her options, the Spirit would prompt her to turn away from things that would harm her or her unborn child, and that she would find us and allow us to adopt her *daughter.* (Linda felt strongly that the child that this unwed birthmother would have would be a girl.) Linda's prayer continued. She asked that we might receive this little girl soon. She asked that we would be selected as adoptive parents *before* we left for graduate school at the end of summer and that we would receive the child this approaching fall!

We have seldom experienced that kind of compassion and spiritual sensitivity. Linda's example of being a true visiting teacher is one that we shall never forget. How could Heavenly Father turn down such an unselfish request? How could Linda have known that, at the very time she was fasting and praying for us, a young woman had just found out that she had conceived out of wedlock? This young girl now found herself having to make one of the hardest and most important decisions in her life. During that soul-searching process, the Spirit guided her to place her unborn child up for adoption through LDS Family Services.

My wife and I continued on our spiritual journey with intense daily prayer. We pled that a birthmother would be inspired to select us as her baby's adoptive parents. We had done all we could do. Now we had to pray and wait and trust. We had no idea how God would cause our road and the road of this birthmother to converge and bring forth the promised blessings. But we were growing ever confident that the roads would converge and that God would bless us. We were soon to find out that he knows and *foreknows* us intimately.

ADOPTION IS ALL ABOUT LOVE

After graduation that summer, we had only a few days to load our belongings in a rented truck and head east to graduate school. Two days before we were to leave, the phone rang. It was our social worker. In a pleasant voice she asked me when we were leaving. In two days, I said. She thanked me and said good-bye. Thinking little of the conversation, I went back to help my wife fill and tape boxes. Then the social worker called again and asked me for our bishop's phone number. As I gave it to her, a sense of excitement began to stir within me. Before I could tell my wife about the call, the social worker called a third time and asked if she could get the phone numbers of the other bishopric members. I was at a loss. We had packed the ward directory in one of the boxes. I ran to a neighbor's apartment to borrow a ward directory and called the social worker with the phone numbers. "Thanks," was all she said, and the conversation ended.

That was it?

My wife and I looked at each other excitedly and said, "Could it be?" Before we had time for further discussion, the phone rang again, and our social worker asked if we could come to her office as soon as possible. We said we would be right there!

At that moment we had a houseful of people loading furniture and boxes into the truck. We made up some lame excuse for leaving and hurried out the door. Soon, we arrived at LDS Family Services in our dirty moving clothes. All of our other clothes were packed! Before we entered the building, we combed our hair in the car mirror, trying to make ourselves look presentable. When we walked inside, we were greeted by our social worker who invited us into her office. She pulled out a blue folder with some papers. She paused, smiled, and said, "You have been selected by a birthmother."

We couldn't believe it! She told us the birthmother's first name and that she was expecting a baby girl during the first part of October! The birthmother had selected us that very day and was told that we were leaving for graduate school. She wanted a face-to-face meeting with us the next day at the LDS Family Services office.

We were speechless. All we could do was hug each other and cry. What an answer to prayer! What a journey it had been! We were going to be parents! It was a miracle! The priesthood blessings, the prayers, the inspiration—it was all real! The Lord was keeping his promises.

Our friends and family were dumbfounded and then they were ecstatic. Just like us, they couldn't believe that we had been selected in a miraculous way that fitted together so many puzzle pieces of recent years.

The following evening at LDS Family Services, we met the birthmother for the first time. We brought her a gift, a small wooden music box that had a window where one could frame a photograph. The music box played the song from the movie *Somewhere in Time*. We also gave the birthmother a single long-stemmed rose with yellow and red tips.

The young woman was beautiful; she seemed to be well-educated, determined, and respectful. She wore a long, plain, gray jumper with a raised waist that fit comfortably over her very pregnant belly. As we sat with her in the room, we tried to memorize everything about her appearance, speech, and mannerisms, knowing that we would likely never see her again. My wife sat close to me and nervously played with my hands. We wanted so badly to make a good impression. We wanted her to see how much we cared for each other and how much we would care for her child. We tried not to give in to our emotions, and at times we were a little lost for words.

The young woman told us a little about how she had selected us as the adoptive couple. She had struggled with the decision and, about halfway through her pregnancy, she had felt impressed to call LDS Family Services. With the help of a social worker, she prayerfully made a list of the things she wanted in an adoptive couple. The social worker then helped her choose six potential couples that fit her criteria. When she saw our portfolio she knew that we were the right couple for her baby. Then she learned that we were leaving for graduate school and asked to quickly have a meeting.

My wife couldn't stop looking at the young woman's stomach. She didn't seem to mind. In fact, she asked if my wife would like to feel the baby. Yes! She guided my wife's hand to her stomach and pointed out the head and the feet. Then the baby moved! My wife smiled and giggled with delight. We appreciated the young woman's sensitivity and invitation to be a part of her experience. We felt impressed to tell her about the priesthood blessing that my father had given us promising that a pregnancy would take place within a year. The birthmother asked when the blessing had been given. When we told her, she smiled and said that the conception would have happened almost exactly as the blessing had stated. It was a big piece of the puzzle that had troubled us for a long time. The Lord had always intended to keep his promise, but we had not known how. When we finally said good-bye, she handed us some ultrasound pictures of the baby—keepsakes of a hope that would arrive in the early autumn, just as our visiting teacher had prayed for.

We had settled in to graduate school now, hundreds of miles from home. Early in October, at about midnight, the phone rang.

We had been anticipating *the call* every day for several weeks. I quickly answered. It was our social worker at LDS Family Services. She said, "I just wanted to let you know that the birthmother has gone into labor and is at the hospital."

No words can express our excitement. I told our social worker that my wife and I would probably leave in the morning to drive home. When I hung up, we talked a little and tried to go to sleep, but it was useless. Finally, my wife nudged me and said, "Let's go now." I agreed. We got up, quickly dressed, packed, and left at 3:30 A.M.

The baby was born early that same morning. That afternoon, we met with our social worker at the LDS Family Services office. As we nervously filled out paperwork, we could hear a little baby's cries in another room. We didn't pay too much attention to the final instructions that our social worker was giving us. Then our social worker left the office and reappeared holding a tiny bundle. She stepped to my wife and placed a beautiful baby girl in her arms. We just stared. We felt so blessed. We had never seen anything so precious and beautiful in our lives. The baby was wearing a little white and pink outfit that her birthmother had picked out. She had wrapped the child in a soft blanket. We couldn't believe that this precious, little girl was ours. She was a miracle.

But the promises of the priesthood blessing were not yet complete. We had been told, "You will have *natural* children." During the adoption process, we hadn't thought much about that part of the blessing. By now, we should have known that with God all things are possible—but we didn't.

Cancer Scare

When our adopted daughter turned one, my wife experienced several sharp pains that doubled her over. As we knelt in prayer to ask the Lord to give her relief, I suddenly received a strong impression that she was in need of urgent medical care. The prayer was followed by a priesthood administration that confirmed my feeling. She should see a doctor . . . now! A swift diagnosis was the promised result. Following the blessing, we both looked at each another and, without question, knew what we should do. We scheduled a quick appointment.

The doctor ordered an ultrasound examination. When the technician began the procedure, she saw a large mass appear on the screen. The technician was obviously taken by surprise and appeared a bit worried. She said the mass looked like a cyst filled with blood and debris. Apparently it had been growing for years.

Beyond concerned, my wife drove home from the appointment intending to call me when she arrived. But just as she walked through the door, the phone rang. It was the doctor, asking if she could return to the lab for an additional blood test to check her chemistries for *cancer!* He said he had scheduled an appointment the next day for her to see an OB/GYN specialist.

Panicked, my wife called me.

Cancer!

I could not keep my mind on my work for the rest of the day. I felt numb and powerless. I searched myself trying to predict an outcome, but my mind was blank.

The next day, the OB/GYN ordered another ultrasound

examination. He thought that the mass was a cyst and judged it to be about the size of a softball. He recommended a surgical procedure called laparoscopy, which involved making a small incision in the abdomen so that he could either test or remove the mass. He wanted to perform the surgery as soon as possible—Tuesday. Because the cyst could erupt at any time, he warned my wife against anything except mild physical activity.

Tuesday arrived. The doctor told us that the operation should last no more than an hour . . . if all went well. I gave my wife a kiss and settled in for what was to be a long wait. I paced. I tried to occupy my mind by reading books. The hour came and went and I became more nervous. I flagged a surgical nurse, but she was not aware of my wife's condition. I paced some more. Another forty-five minutes ticked off the clock. Finally the surgeon, dressed from head to foot in green operating scrubs, came into the waiting room. He ushered me into a little consultation room. The first thing he said was, "Your wife is doing fine and we are just about finished." He said that they had found a much larger mass than expected. When he saw it, he said, his heart sank. He was sure it was a malignant ovarian tumor. He had little choice except to make a long incision and remove the mass. Then he had ordered that the mass be tested for malignancy. To his relief it was not malignant. Rather, it was a ball of endometriosis about the size of a small cantaloupe. He explained that endometria tissue lines the uterus. Endometriosis occurs when the tissue grows outside the uterus where it does not belong. Then it can affect internal tissues and organs, cause large cysts, and result in infertility. The endometriosis had damaged one of my wife's ovaries beyond repair, and he had had to remove it. The other ovary had also been damaged, but he felt he could save it. Then the surgeon pinched his fingers together so that only a tiny gap separated them. He said, "I came *this* close to doing a full hysterectomy on your wife."

I stared at him blankly. I couldn't believe the seriousness of my wife's condition. I was shocked to hear the doctor use words such as *cancer, endometriosis,* and *hysterectomy.* I remembered the strong prompting that I had received in prayer and during the priesthood blessing that she should seek medical care immediately. The surgeon said that any further delay could have resulted in the cyst's bursting, the second ovary's being damaged beyond hope, and his having to perform a full hysterectomy.

Reeling from the news, I was escorted to my wife's room. I steeled myself. She was just waking from the anesthetic and knew nothing about what I had been told. I sat in a chair beside her hospital bed and held her hand. I asked how she was feeling. "Tired," she mumbled. She was awake but still groggy. She was beginning to feel the pain of the surgery. I didn't want to tell her the news, but the recovery room nurses had told her about the large incision in her belly. She asked me, "I wonder why?"

I took a deep breath and began to explain. When I came to the part about removing one ovary and having to repair the other, she squeezed her eyes shut and a single tear rolled down her cheek. She held my hand tightly and said nothing.

RECOVERY AND LUPRON

The recovery period was long and painful. My wife needed help for simple, everyday tasks. She was tired and weak and was restricted from lifting heavy objects. Several weeks after the surgery, she began to experience severe pains in and around her incision whenever she tried to get up or lie down. The pain brought her to tears. She dreaded using the bathroom at night or even trying to lie down because the pain was so terrible. I felt helpless. I could do nothing to alleviate her discomfort. She slipped into a deep sadness as she struggled to deal with the loss of her ovary. The endometriosis was still a problem. Although the tumor had been removed, the endometriosis still existed and threatened to grow back and cause her further harm. Soon, she was told, she would need to begin an aggressive treatment of Lupron shots to retard the growth and to "burn out" all the existing microscopic endometrium. She would be injected with this drug once a month for six months. The treatment would force her body into a temporary menopause-like state, and she would have to endure the difficult side effects.

During those dark days, our little adopted daughter was our one delight. We were so happy with her, but we also felt sad because endometriosis is usually synonymous with infertility. The chances of our producing a natural child had been slim to nonexistent with my low fertility score. Now that my wife had lost one ovary and the other had been badly damaged, now that her body was filled with endometriosis and Lupron would shortly propel her into menopause, our chances were nil. But we weren't thinking much about the future. Our attention was centered on recovery from the operation and gearing up for the upcoming Lupron treatment. By now we had dismissed the promised blessing that we would one day achieve a pregnancy and have a natural child. For the moment we had forgotten the miraculous events that had surrounded the adoption of our daughter. There were no more miracles for us, we thought; we just prayed for the ability to endure.

The clock was ticking. Within a few days, my wife would complete her final menstrual period, and shortly thereafter she would be scheduled to receive her first Lupron shot . . . and the menopause would begin.

The day came. Before the doctor gave my wife the initial Lupron injection, he explained that she could expect side effects such as weight gain, bloating, nausea, and fatigue. The sudden halt of hormones would likely also cause depression. An irony would be that the side effects mimic pregnancy.

Depression and Weight Gain

Time passed slowly. Winter had set in. We had only one car, which was old and continually in need of repairs. My employment situation was rocky. My hours were insufficient to support the family. I had to work late into the evening to make ends meet. Our medical bills were strangling our already tight budget. Our bishop offered to help us, but we decided to wait, hoping that the Lord would recognize our sacrifices and tithes, and that he would provide a way for us to keep meeting our basic needs. During that long, cold winter my wife was often home alone, doing her best to tend our daughter, recuperate from her surgery, and endure the side effects of Lupron.

She became deeply depressed. Many days, she would cry on my shoulder, frustrated with how she was feeling and sad that she could not shake off the dark melancholy. She still grieved the loss of her ovary. She thought she was failing as a mother. She hated how she looked. Just as the doctor had predicted, she was gaining weight and was bloated. She had always prided herself in being physically fit, and now, to combat the weight gain and to try and flatten out her stomach, she resumed her six-day-a-week regimen of arising early and working out in the gym. But no matter how hard she tried, she was not able to control her weight; she was gaining five pounds a month. When she ate she was nauseated, but she was hungry all the time. To make matters worse, people began to notice her bloated stomach and ask her when the baby was due. What could she say? *I'm not having a baby! I can't have a baby! I'm just fat!*

She became more depressed. When she went to the doctor to get her monthly Lupron shot, she complained about the weight gain, bloating, and nausea. She always received the same answer: "It's the Lupron. Everything will begin to return to normal when the treatment ends." The doctor prescribed some hormonal pills to reduce the symptoms. But nothing worked, and she kept gaining more weight. She doubled her efforts at the gym. The pounds and bloating increased. We would have to accept the fact all we could do was pray and wait out the remainder of the six months of Lupron—months filled with more fat, bloating, nausea, fatigue, and depression.

Finally, the last Lupron shot was imminent. My wife's stomach had now become so stretched and bloated that she would experience muscle spasms. One night, as we were sitting on the couch, I looked at her stomach and saw a large, wave-like ripple start at the top of her belly and run to the bottom. I gasped and stared. I had never seen such a muscle spasm before. She looked at me and said hopelessly, "I know! My stomach is large and stretched out, and I have been having these spasms for several weeks!"

This was intolerable! We had to get our lives back. We would be so grateful when the Lupron shots ended so that she could begin to feel better and start losing the weight.

PARTING THE RED SEA

A few weeks later, my wife received the last shot. She would have to wait another thirty days for the drug to wear off and for hormones to surface and begin to circulate normally through her system. When the thirty-day mark arrived, the doctor wanted to see her again. This was to be a big event for our family. The long ordeal was finally over, and we would get Mom back. So all three of us piled into the car and drove to the check-up.

My wife had prepared a long list of questions to ask the doctor, most of which had to do with her weight, her hard belly, and when she could expect to feel normal again. As the doctor began examining her, she peppered him with questions. He didn't seem to be listening. Rather, he was focusing on her hard stomach. This wasn't normal.

"Yes, I know!" she said, sounding frustrated. "That is what I've been trying to tell you these last months!"

Suddenly, he exited the room, and we just looked at each other, perplexed. Soon a nurse walked in. She said that the doctor wanted my wife to receive an ultrasound immediately. We didn't know what was going on. (Later, we learned that the doctor feared that another tumor had developed.) I picked up our daughter and followed my wife to the ultrasound room.

When my wife lay down on the ultrasound table, the technician, not knowing our situation, looked kindly at our little girl, and asked, "Are Mommy and Daddy going to look at the baby?" She pointed at my wife's bloated stomach.

My wife quickly corrected her. She was not pregnant, she said. She was just bloated from the Lupron treatments. The nurse looked embarrassed and simply said, "Oh." Then she began the exam. After a few moments she paused and stared at the screen with the look of puzzlement. Then she said, "You're pregnant."

My wife said, "No, I'm not. The doctor is just worried about my bloated stomach."

The nurse said, "Yes, you are pregnant."

My wife firmly replied, "No, I'm not pregnant." Then she pointed at our one-year-old daughter. "Our little girl is adopted. We can't have natural children."

The nurse said, "Well, you're pregnant. Look!"

She pivoted the screen toward us, and there, right before our eyes was a baby's face. My jaw dropped. My wife began to cry. We couldn't speak. Dumbfounded, we watched this little miracle bob around on the screen.

How? Why? When? Too many questions. This was beyond logic. If we hadn't had proof right before our eyes, we wouldn't have believed it. Who could?

The nurse immediately began the standard checks for abnormalities and to take measurements. The child was a little girl, 6½ months along . . . and perfect. As though we were trying to talk the nurse out of it, we told her about my severe infertility. We told her about my wife's endometriosis. We told her about losing an ovary and the other being damaged. We told her about the Lupron shots, and how my wife had begun receiving them only days after her last menstrual period. We told her that it was impossible to achieve a pregnancy.

We all laughed. We all cried. The nurse began to call the baby "your little miracle." Soon, news spread through the entire clinic, and suddenly a tremendous cheer went up from all the staff. The shocked doctor told us that such a thing occurring was right up there with Moses parting the Red Sea.

Twelve weeks later, I watched my wife give birth to a beautiful, healthy baby girl. We named her Grace, which fittingly means *God's Blessing*.

GOD'S BLESSINGS

My wife and I do not fully understand why our two little girls came to us in such a miraculous manner. They are like two witnesses of a single truth: If God can do this, he can do anything.

We know that miracles are often explained away as "good science" or "lucky." But we know that any explanation outside of giving full credit to God would be offensive to him. We know that God is a God of miracles and that he keeps his promises. We live with indisputable proof.

We look back on those confusing, discouraging, and turbulent years, and can now bear solemn and unwavering testimony that the Lord was with us every step of the way. Though we were unaware of his involvement at the time, we can now see that he was extending his divine help and guiding us through a complicated maze of twists and turns. He showed us his incredible power. We were always in his consciousness. We were always loved.

❧

Is any thing too hard for the Lord?

GENESIS 18:14